Selling
Through
Negotiation

Dedicated to my wife,
MILDRED
and to our children
BARBARA
DAVID
LOUISE
NANCY and
ROBERT
who were practicing
effective sales negotiation techniques
on me and each other
long before I thought about
writing this book.

Selling Through Negotiation

The HANDBOOK of Sales Negotiation

Homer B. Smith

American Management Association

This book is available at a special
discount when ordered in bulk quantities.
For information, contact Special Sales Department,
AMACOM, a division of American Management Association,
135 West 50th Street, New York, NY 10020.

Library of Congress Cataloging-in-Publication Data

Smith, Homer B., 1915–
    Selling through negotiation.

    Bibliography: p.
    1. Selling. 2. Negotiation in business. I. Title.
[HF5438.25.S64 1988]   658.8'1   88–16818
ISBN 0-8144-7707 (pbk.)

© *1988* **Homer B. Smith**
All rights reserved.
Printed in the United States of America.

Printing number

10   9   8   7   6   5   4   3   2

Contents

PART II: Combining Your Negotiating and Selling Skills to Close More Sales

PART III: Increasing Your Questioning and Listening Skills

Epilogue

Introduction

THOSE of us who have been training salespeople over the years have been impressed by the recent growth of books and seminars on negotiation skills. Like most people, we used to think of "negotiation" as an activity engaged in primarily by government diplomats, financiers and by labor and management officials to settle differences across a bargaining table.

Now we realize that since the very beginning of commerce, salespeople have been negotiators, too. They had to negotiate with prospects and customers to arrive at a mutually acceptable sale of their products or services.

Thanks to the authors of the books on negotiation who identified the basic strategies, we now realize that salespeople can improve their total selling skills by combining negotiating techniques with their conventional skills of communication and persuasion.

Unfortunately, the emphasis in current books and courses on negotiation is primarily on making better BUYERS rather than better SALESPEOPLE. In fact, you could come away from a negotiation seminar with the feeling that you have been overhearing a game plan your potential customers intend to put into play when you make your next sales call. We still recommend that salespeople read one or more of the books on general negotiation and attend a negotiation workshop when available. Salespeople are also consumers, spouses, parents and members of society. Using the techniques of effective negotiation will be helpful to all of us in dealing with many of life's person-to-person encounters.

How to Cope With Buyers Who Have Taken a Course in Negotiations

Section

One great advantage salespeople gain in learning about negotiation techniques is exposure to the strategies and tactics a buyer who has taken the course will probably use on them. Once these are anticipated, and workable methods for coping with them are devised, the salesperson has a much better chance of coming out of the sales negotiations with a profitable order.

Chapter 2 is devoted exclusively to helping the salesperson identify and cope with the negotiation tactics professional buyers are apt to use on them.

Some firms send their salespeople to negotiation seminars because they feel that a general knowledge of negotiation skills will be helpful. The best results have been obtained, however, when the sales training executives of these firms take the additional step of relating specific negotiation strategies to the SELLING side of the negotiation situation.

It was the experience of these sales trainers, shared with the author, that demonstrated the need for this book to assist salespeople and sales trainers in making the transition.

Selling Requires Specific Negotiation Skills

In this book, we discuss negotiating skills as they relate to selling skills. Then we show how the combined skills can be used more effectively by salespeople.

To do this, we pull out of the broad area of negotiation those specific strategies and tactics that are especially valuable for salespeople.

Meanwhile, we show how these negotiating skills can supplement and strengthen the effectiveness of the modern professional selling skills that are based on communication and persuasion.

PART I: DEVELOPING YOUR SALES NEGOTIATION SKILLS

The first four Chapters will prepare salespeople for negotiation in selling. The negotiation strategies and tactics salespeople can use in dealing with prospects and customers are identified and explained along with examples of their application to selling.

Salespeople and buyers both have advantages going into the typical sales negotiation. These are identified and explained along with suggestions on how salespeople can make use of their existing negotiation strength and develop additional power.

In Chapter 2, the negotiation tactics that professional buyers are learning to use when dealing with salespeople are identified and interpreted. Suggestions are given on ways in which the salesperson can recognize these tactics and cope with them.

At all times, the discussion is based on achieving an outcome that is mutually beneficial for BOTH the salesperson and customer . . . the traditional Win-Win result.

PART II: INTEGRATING YOUR NEGOTIATING
AND SELLING SKILLS

Starting with Chapter 5, and in the remaining Chapters, we integrate the most effective selling techniques used by today's professional salespeople at each stage of the sale with the new concept of selling through negotiation. Experienced salespeople will recognize the professional persuasive selling techniques readily, but will appreciate having them tailored to and reinforced by the strategies and tactics of sales negotiation.

For beginning salespeople, this is a great opportunity to learn the best techniques used by modern professional salespeople, integrated for the first time with those negotiating skills that are most effective for use by salespeople.

PART III: INCREASING YOUR QUESTIONING
AND LISTENING SKILLS

Good sales negotiators use probing questions to get prospects and customers to express their needs, desires and prejudices. Once these are uncovered by skillful questioning, the right decisions become more obvious for both the salesperson and the prospect.

Asking questions does little good unless the salesperson listens to the answers and sifts them effectively for clues to guide the sales negotiation in the right direction.

Good listening also involves observing the prospect's body language to interpret problems as well as buying signals.

Asking probing questions and listening are skills professional salespeople use in all the steps of the sales negotiation. While specific uses for questions are suggested where appropriate in Chapters 7 through 10, we cover questioning and listening skills separately in Part III for special emphasis.

A HANDBOOK FOR SALES NEGOTIATION

We cannot cover all of the background or the many uses for good negotiation techniques that are covered so well in the general texts and workshops on negotiation. Instead, we have concentrated on those techniques that are used primarily in buying and selling situations.

We recommend that this book be used, as the title suggests, as a handbook for Selling Through Negotiation, supplemented by one or more of the good books on general negotiation available in your library or bookstore.

Sales Trainers Know the Importance of Negotiating Skills

The author gives special credit to members of the National Society of Sales Training Executives, top sales trainers of companies with national distribution, who shared their experiences in tailoring available material on negotiation techniques to selling situations, read and commented on drafts of the chapters, and who supported the need for this book to help salespeople and trainers make more effective use of negotiating skills.

It is an honor to have been a member of NSSTE for many years and a Past President of a group which is willing to share their experiences and expertise in training top salespeople.

PART I:

Developing Your Sales Negotiation Skills

1

The Negotiation Approach to Selling

Selling is Negotiating

DOWN through the ages, selling and negotiating have gone hand in hand. Seldom did the traders for merchandise or services agree on the first offer to buy or sell. Haggling became a universal language long before it got the more respectable title of "negotiation."

In America, our marketing sophistication with its take-it-or-leave-it pricing of products has greatly reduced price negotiation in retail stores. But as travelers to other countries know, merchants still expect the customers to negotiate (haggle) over the prices in the local markets. Travelers who are unwilling to negotiate or are not aware that they can, end up paying more than they should.

Thanks to the authors of the books on negotiation, however, more of the buying public is becoming aware that negotiation is possible.

Negotiation skills until recently were generally considered to be those skills used at high levels, primarily by government diplomats and by labor and management officials across a bargaining table.

They were the skills needed by government negotiators to get the best part of any treaties or marketing agreements for their respective countries. They were the skills used by top-level labor and management negotiators to achieve a fair settlement at the bargaining table. They were the skills needed by lawyers pitted against other lawyers and judges to get the best of an agreement or sentence for their clients.

Buyers Learning Negotiating Techniques

In recent years, however, thanks to the authors of books and leaders of seminars and workshops on negotiation, consumers are learning to use negotiation skills at personal levels like buying a home, a car, a major appliance or even to get a new job or promotion. They are learning how to get a "better deal" from the sellers.

Professional buyers like purchasing agents for business firms have long used the principles of negotiation to get the best "deal" for their companies from the suppliers. Few recognized the skills they had as part of the realm of negotiation, however. The buying techniques were usually picked up through experience in "wheeling and dealing" along with the general courses on purchasing. In recent years, however, professional buyers and people looking forward to a career in purchasing began to read books and attend seminars on basic negotiation.

Professional Buyers Attending Negotiation Seminars

Business firms now send their purchasing department personnel and developing executives to negotiation seminars to help them learn to negotiate better terms with suppliers.

Many firms go beyond the negotiation workshops for their purchasing staff and send them to workshops designed for salespeople! One can assume that learning persuasive selling skills is valuable for anyone. But sending buyers to sales workshops to learn what salespeople are taught reminds one of the practice of coaches sending observers to a competitor's practice field.

What Do Salespeople Get From General Negotiation Programs?

How does the salesperson benefit from the new books and seminars on negotiation? As a consumer, great! But while reading the typical book or attending a workshop on negotiation, the typical salesperson soon gets the feeling that most of the strategies covered are designed to help buyers get the best deal from salespeople or sellers.

Certainly, knowing what the professional buyers are learning about negotiating better prices and terms can be most helpful to salespeople. As in sporting events, it always helps to know what the competitor is up to.

Some business firms, particularly those who sell through bidding on construction jobs or large supply contracts, send their salespeople to general negotiation workshops to alert them to the strategies and tactics they are apt to face from the professional buyers.

Alert salespeople are able to evaluate the various negotiation principles described in the books and workshops in order to apply them to their own sales presentations. They are also alerted to the tactics recommended to the consumers for getting better terms from salespeople and can develop defenses against them. But progressive sales executives have found that they get better results when they have their sales training departments develop their own courses on negotiation, tailoring the basic negotiation concepts to the salesperson's advantage.

That's Why This Book Was Written

That is the purpose of this book . . . to show how salespeople can combine the principles of negotiation with their existing selling skills to increase their sales success.

The author is a former national sales trainer for a manufacturer of business machines and a past president of the National Society of Sales Training Executives.

It is from this background of knowing what professional sales trainers need to do to better equip their salespeople to use the negotiation skills and to cope with buyers who have taken courses in negotiation that this book was developed.

Salespeople Have Always Been Negotiators

Professional salespeople have always been negotiators whether they realized it or not.

All of the selling skills, product knowledge, attitudes and working habits developed during a salesperson's career are aimed at developing greater negotiating power for the salesperson when in a sales situation.

Professional Buyers Are Negotiators

Professional buyers are also negotiators whether they have taken a negotiation course or not.

They expect to negotiate with the salespeople of suppliers to get the most satisfactory solution possible in the final purchase.

When the buyer and seller have comparable power going into the negotiation, and comparable skills in negotiation, the result is a sale and a purchase that is usually satisfactory to both parties.

Everyone is a Negotiator

Everyone has to negotiate to survive in life. Some are better than others whether from natural ability or experience.

Most of us have had experience like this either as a nine-year-old or as a parent. "Hey, Mom. Can I go to the movies?" "Not until you mow the lawn!" "Gee, Mom. The kids want to go right after lunch. I'll mow the lawn right after I get back, okay?" "All right, but you be sure you get the lawn mowed before your Dad gets home." "Right!" That's negotiation in a simple but highly effective form.

Negotiation skills begin early in life without any formal instruction. Most parents can relate to this situation. Parent tries to take a small tool away from Baby because she might hurt herself. Baby holds tight and comes back with a counter offer, "Waaaaaaa!" Parent makes a concession and counter offer, "Okay, okay! Take it then! But don't put it in your mouth or I'll spank you."

Was this a learning experience in negotiation for Baby? Since you have been a negotiator of sorts all your life, when you are exposed to some negotiation strategy or tactic in this book, you're bound to say to yourself from time to time, "Hey, what's new? That's happened to me many times." or, "Right. I've done that before and it really works." The trouble is, if you're the typical salesperson, you didn't put it all together at the right time and in the right place to make it work for you in a selling situation. We'll try to remedy that and prepare you to become a good negotiator by using the same strategies and tactics in your selling that the good negotiators use in other fields . . . including buying.

Negotiation In Selling

Even though buyers and sellers have been negotiating since the dawn of commerce, the specific skills of negotiation have been overlooked in the texts and courses designed for the training and development of salespeople. When specific training programs were first developed for salespeople, they consisted almost entirely of product knowledge. (Unfortunately, too many courses still do.) Later, sales trainers added formulas for techniques like making a demonstration, overcoming objections and closing the sale.

Over the years, authors and trainers elaborated on the formulas and added more techniques designed to encourage the customers to buy.

In more recent years, the emphasis shifted to a determination of the physical and emotional reasons why people buy, their "buying motives." Salespeople now identify the benefits the buyers will enjoy from the specific selling features of the product or service.

If the salesperson can detect which buying motives are strongest in a particular prospect, he or she will emphasize those benefits which will best satisfy that buying motive.

So today, the principles of good communication and persuasion have become an important part of sales training to help the salesperson lead the prospect into making the buying decision.

Sure, we know there is still high-pressure, competitive selling going on. Salespeople and buyers are still entering the arena to do battle where one wins and the other loses. But with the growth of professionalism and sophistication in both buying and selling in recent years, the buyer and seller relationships have become more and more a negotiation exercise. The strategies of the professional negotiators are being practiced by both parties so that both come out with a sale that is acceptable.

Ideally, this is the Win-Win situation. The buyer gets his or her money's worth and the seller gets a reasonable profit or income.

Salespeople Need Skill In Negotiating

Sales training professionals are becoming aware that the negotiating skills once thought practical only in top level confrontations of diplomats or management and labor excutives, also have their place in the day to day sales situations every salesperson faces.

So the questions become:

1. Which negotiation strategies are applicable to selling?

2. How do these strategies differ from those now being taught to salespeople?

3. What does the salesperson need to know to be able to cope with professional buyers who are trained in negotiation skills?

4. How do the skills of communication and persuasion fit into negotiation activity?

These are some of the questions that will be answered as we go along.

The Win-Win Concept in Sales Negotiation

The ideal attitude in sales negotiation, and the one most prevailing at the professional levels, is that the buyer and the salesperson must become partners in arriving at solutions rather than adversaries or competitors. Whatever the outcome, it must be mutually beneficial for both parties. This is often referred to as a "Win-win" buying and selling strategy.

In the effective customer-salesperson working partnership, each partner is willing to accommodate the other, to help each other win a fair share, to tie their future successes together. Out of such negotiated sales, one can expect close and continuing good customer and salesperson relationships.

Negotiation as partners assumes that both the customer and the salesperson are equals. Each partner may have favorable power in one circumstance or another, but on average, the best negotiation strategy is to have the power of the parties stay in reasonable balance.

The Salesperson Becomes an Adviser

When sales negotiation is used in its ideal form, the salesperson takes on the role of a consultant or adviser.

When such negotiation is effective, the customer relies on the salesperson to provide the solutions to the customer's needs and to solve problems or to better conditions. The salesperson obviously can benefit from this

R.E. has 2 customers

kind of relationship and should work toward keeping it intact though acceptable performance.

Professional Buyers are the "Good Guys"

When one thinks of negotiation in the broad sense, there is the temptation to think of it in an adversary relationship like a contest where one party is victorious, the other defeated. In sales negotiation, however, the desired result is that both parties win. The salesperson wins a sale and profit for his or her firm. The buyer wins a purchase that will increase profit, reduce loss or make life easier and happier.

While every experienced salesperson can give examples of prospects and customers who love to make life miserable for salespeople, they will usually agree that most buyers are reasonable people. They have a job to do and want to do it well. Their assignment is to get the "best deal" for their respective firms, and if they don't, they'll soon be looking for another job.

The so-called "best deal," while related to price, is not necessarily the lowest price in every instance. Professional buyers understand that final cost and total benefits are more important considerations than raw price and will negotiate with salespeople on this basis.

If the salesperson is unable to persuade the buyer during the negotiation that it will be to his or her ultimate advantage to pay more for a product or service because of additional, identified benefits, the buyer has every right and even the obligation to buy from someone else who offers a lower price for a comparable package.

PERSUASION VS NEGOTIATION

When does persuasion leave off and negotiation start in a typical sales situation?

Before we accept the logical response, "Who cares?", we should try to recognize some distinctions between these two important tools of selling in order to make both work more effectively.

Professional salespeople who study the material on negotiation soon recognize many of the techniques and principles they are already using. Persuasion and negotiation go hand in hand.

There are no indicator lights that flash in one color when persuasion is going on and in another color when negotiation occurs. If there were such lights, they would probably flicker back and forth during a typical sales call and both would be on part of the time. At a given moment, one party can be attempting to persuade the other to accept a point while the other is negotiating for an alternative solution.

Every negotiator uses persuasion to get the other party to accept the proposal currently being offered. The labor representative tries to persuade management to accept the latest offer, outlining the benefits that would occur if that happens. The management representative uses persuasion to establish the benefits of accepting the company's offer.

Where Does Sales Negotiation Begin?

Salespeople call on their persuasion strategies in the early stages of the sale, the approach and the initial presentation. They also depend upon persuasion whenever there is resistance to the conditions of the sale. This occurs throughout the sale.

Finally, salespeople must persuade the prospect to accept the proposal, to close the sale.

We might say that negotiation enters the selling scene at any point where persuasion has stalled, where the salesperson and buyer have not agreed on a common goal and some give and take is needed.

Certainly when the prospect is asked to buy and refuses or shows indecision, the salesperson has to add negotiation strategies as well as persuasion to the selling situation.

The exception to this generality is found in getting the appointment. The salesperson frequently has to resort to negotiation to get an appointment and then to get agreement on the date and time.

The salesperson asks a prospect for a Thursday appointment but gets this reply, "No, I'll be out of town Thursday." Now the salesperson starts to negotiate. "Would Friday morning be convenient?" "No, I have appointments all morning." "How about Friday afternoon, say at two?" "Let me see. Can you make it three instead?" "Yes, that would be fine. I'll be there at three on Friday, Mr. Roberts."

The salesperson, through negotiation tactics, got an appointment after being refused. No amount of persuasion alone would have convinced the prospect to grant the initial request for a Thursday appointment.

Negotiation Closes the Sale

Negotiation involves an exchange of points of view. In selling, the salesperson and the buyer have both agreements and disagreements on points of view. Through persuasion and negotiation, when these points of view come together, a sale usually results.

Negotiation AFTER the Sale

Most salespeople depend upon developing a line of loyal customers for continued success and territory development. Inevitably there will be problems to resolve and conflicts to settle that would otherwise jeopardize the relationship.

The salesperson has to depend on good negotiation skills to bring the conflicting points of view into a mutually satisfactory settlement.

SELLING AND NEGOTIATING ARE INSEPARABLE

Selling and negotiating are obviously quite compatible. In fact, they are usually inseparable in commercial and industrial selling. Those of us who have been in sales for a reasonable time realize that we have been using some of the accepted negotiation strategies all along. We just gave them other names.

Now that negotiation techniques have been brought down from the high levels of give and take to the everyday buyer's world, we find that there are some good techniques used by the professional negotiators that should be added to those already in use in the selling profession.

As we become aware that prospects and customers in growing numbers are receiving training in professional negotiation skills, there is an initial impulse to consider them as adversaries or opponents. The unknown is usually frightening and we become defensive. Yet this new era of negotiating skills development has actually made the relationship between professional buyers and salespeople better.

Sales Negotiation is Like a Game!

Selling is frequently referred to as "the selling game." This description is probably not fair in describing the professionalism which modern selling has become.

But there are many aspects of selling which liken it to any professional game. The same is true of basic negotiation. So when you put them both together in sales negotiation, it may be helpful to at least compare the planning and performance as a game.

In sales negotiation there are players, the buyer and the seller, there are rules to be observed, there are strategies for offense and defense, and the players require knowledge and skill to succeed with their part in the sales negotiation.

Unlike the usual games where there has to be an obvious winner, however, the successful sales negotiation "game" has to come out with both sides winners. This is true in any kind of selling, however. It's referred to as the win-win situation where both parties are satisfied with the outcome.

For most of this book, like coaches for winning teams, we'll be working on OFFENSE, discussing the negotiation strategies and tactics that work especially well for salespeople. Then we will integrate these negotiation skills into the basic stages of the successful sale and combine them with existing persuasive skills.

But first, let's start with ways to develop an effective DEFENSE, how to cope with buyers who have taken courses in negotiation.

2

How to Cope with Buyer Negotiation Tactics

Defense! Defense!

MANY football games have been won because the defensive team was able to read the other team's offensive tactics and be at the right spot at the right time with the right defensive move to prevent a score. Sure, the offense makes the touchdowns and field goals needed to score, but the game is won only if the defense keeps the opponent from scoring more.

Defense is just as important in individual contests like tennis. Your own points don't win the match unless you can prevent the opponent from scoring more.

In sales negotiation as in sports, having a good defense against the buyer's negotiation tactics is just as important as the salesperson's own negotiating power.

Those professional buyers who have taken courses in negotiation have a stronger offense for the game of buying because of the strategies they have learned for getting a better deal from salespeople. Unless you understand what those strategies are and have developed a defense for them, you are much more apt to come out on the short end of the score . . . the final sale!

BUYER STRATEGIES IN SALES NEGOTIATION

Before we discuss the negotiation strategies and tactics that salespeople can apply to their sales situations, their OFFENSE, let's concentrate on DEFENSE! The boxing coach gives trainees lessons on avoiding the

Rationale
for learning
to respond
to tactics

punches delivered their way and how to turn them to advantage. Without that defensive skill, the trainee may not be around long enough to benefit from the rest of the training.

Without an understanding of the "punches" coming your way from the buyer with negotiating skills, you have much less of an opportunity to apply the skills that improve your own negotiating chances.

Win-win or Win-lose?

We have previously discussed the "partner" or "win-win" concept in sales negotiation where both the buyer and the salesperson win. This is the ideal sales negotiation outcome and the one achieved most of the time.

We will stress this in our future discussions of sales negotiation strategies and tactics.

But the salesperson must be prepared for the occasional win-lose buyer just as buyers must be prepared for the occasional win-lose seller. In this section we will recognize and discuss the handling of buyer negotiation tactics without moralizing on their use.

Some will be used by professional buyers who will be satisfied with a win-win outcome but want to make sure they will get the best terms possible.

The techniques for coping with the tactics are the same regardless of the buyer's attitude, and if successful, the final outcome will be the desired win-win relationship.

When the typical win-lose, tough-buying negotiator finds that the salesperson is not taken in by the tactics and obviously knows what is going on, the buyer will usually back off and settle for the win-win result. Some buyers like the game they play so well that, like professional athletes, they even have more respect for the salesperson who is able to match negotiation wits with them.

24 TACTICS BUYERS USE ON SALESPEOPLE AND HOW TO COPE WITH THEM

Let's discuss some of the tactics used by buyers during the sales negotiation and what you can do to cope with them. They are given here in no particular order of importance.

1. The Extreme Initial Demand. One of the best recognition signals for the win-lose buyer is the extreme initial demand. "We won't pay over $3.18 a pound delivered to our warehouse."

The salesperson is protected against this approach by knowing market conditions and prices so as not to get sucked into a bidding war with the competitors. The approach is to treat the statement like other price objections which are covered in Chapter 9, moving on the assumption that the prospect is not aware of current market prices.

2. The Budget Limitation or Bogey Tactic. Before buying most things, people have a maximum amount in mind that they will pay. Businesses and families call this a budget figure. In negotiations, it is sometimes referred to as a "bogey," a word the dictionary says is used to identify "a numerical standard of performance."

The budget or bogey sets a limit to what the buyer can pay for an item or a program and this is often brought out by the buyer in sales negotiation as an excuse to get the salesperson to make concessions. "Your proposal is just what we want, but our budget for the whole installation is only $10,000."

The budget limitation tactic is entirely ethical, often true, and can actually work effectively for both the buyer and the salesperson.

Budgets are usually established for purchasing costly products or service or large quantities. Government agencies announce their budget limits for a new building. An office manager tells the machine salesperson that the proposed price would exceed the departmental allocation for new equipment.

One of the advantages of the legitimate budget limitations or bogey is that it becomes a common obstacle for both the buyer and the salesperson so they can try to work out the problem together. The buyer says she likes the product, so the negotiations start on a friendly basis.

The only way to go now is for the salesperson to take a fresh look at the customer's needs and make suggestions on things that can be trimmed or substituted to get the price down to the budget. Often the budget can be upgraded by the salesperson who does a good job of educating the customer to the advantages of spending a little more to get a better return on the investment.

Of course, some claims of budget limitations are just a ruse to test the price offered by the salesperson. The tactic works effectively for the customer because it tends to force the salesperson down to the best possible terms.

Coping with the Bogey Tactics

Here are some ways to cope with the budget limitation or bogey tactics of prospects and customers.

a. Make sure that the bogey is real. Check it out for flexibility if it proves to be legitimate.

b. Anticipate the budget resistance and do your homework on alternatives to your primary proposal that would reduce the price.

c. When presenting alternatives to reduce cost, point out the disadvantages as well. Be careful not to run down the alternative so much that the prospect will not consider it at its lower cost. Stress that the alternative is still a good buy for what it will cost. A lower priced sale is better than none at all!

d. Try to negotiate a different time frame if some budget items can be carried over into another budget period. "Let's do this much under your present budget and leave this part until next quarter."

e. If you suspect that the person who brings up the budget restrictions is not the final decision-maker, find out who is and test the limits of the budget figure with that person after stressing the benefits of exceeding it.

f. Ask the buyer what he or she is willing to do to help reduce the cost of the purchase. "Would you be willing to do the interior painting yourself if we could get the price down to your budget figure?"

If you can prepare ahead of time for a possible budget restriction, you can usually come away with the sale while competitors are doing nothing to cope with it or are taking too much time thinking about possible alternatives.

Bargaining chips for the Bogey

Budget restrictions that keep the prospect from buying can actually help the salesperson who is prepared with some "bargaining chips" that the competition hasn't thought about. Here are some examples.

"I think we could keep within your budget . . .

a. if you agree to buy all your supplies from us for a year."
b. if you can use our stock model instead of the one specified on the bid sheet."
c. if you can give us an advance payment of $5,000."
d. if you order a hundred cases at a time."
e. if we can make delivery by the end of the month."
f. if we also get the contract for the carpeting."
g. if you agree to do the uncrating and set-up."

You can add more alternatives to this list from your own experience with other sales and contracts and the normal conditions relative to your product or service.

3. "You Gotta Do Better Than That". Salespeople with active competitors and a fairly uniform product like fuel oil or printing paper get used to having some buyers react to the offered price with, "You gotta do better than that, Charlie." For some professional buyers, in fact, this is an automatic form of resistance.

On the surface, this might sound like a very friendly thing to do. The buyer is saying that he would like to buy from you but your price is higher than some other bids. All you have to do is lower the price a bit, right?

The trouble with this buyer tactic, usually, is that the same pained and troubled remark is made to all the bidders, even the low ones. Smart buyers know that there is some leeway in the prices of highly competitive products and this is one way to get to the bottom line.

The problem with this tactic in the long run, however, is that the competitive salespeople soon recognize its use and add a comfortable cushion to the first price offered. It also leads to a lowering of quality and service and selling becomes one of price alone.

First defense is knowing your price

The first defense for the "You gotta do better" tactic is to know your price and how to defend it.

In most selling situations, some competitor is always able to sell at a lower price by cutting something out. Find out what the difference is, then follow the usual techniques for defending the price and showing how it is the total value received and the total cost involved that is most important, NOT the raw price. See Chapter 9 for suggestions.

If it turns out that the buyer has a good case, and you may have to lower your price, try to get some concession in return. Ask for the order on the spot if you do such-and-such. Offer the lowered price with another condition like an order for other items or a year's supply. Expect price pressure, plan for it and be ready to act.

4. Time Pressures and Deadlines. Professional buyers know the power of time pressure and deadlines to get salespeople to make concessions. Sometimes these can be used to advantage by salespeople to stir up their own management to make concessions.

Sample buyer pressure statements.

Here are some ways in which buyers use the deadline tactic to get the best proposal quickly. You can no doubt add more from your own experience.

a. "Our budget expires the first of the month, so we will need to get your best price before then."

b. "I need your final offer to take to the staff meeting tomorrow morning."

c. "The bids will be opened next Monday morning at 10 o'clock."

d. "I'm going to check the prices of the Johnson Company tomorrow."

e. "Charles Walters will take over as buyer of maintenance supplies starting the first of the month and he will have some ideas of his own on suppliers."

f. "The boss is leaving for a six-weeks tour of Europe tomorrow and he has to approve the order."

g. "The buying committee meets next Monday. Is that the proposal you want them to review?"

h. "We start production on May 1st. If you can't get your material to us before then, we'll have to get it from Foster and Bailey."

Buyers obviously have legitimate deadlines, too, whether real or self-imposed. The salesperson's objective should be to test those deadlines by trying to change them if that is important in getting the sale.

As mentioned before, the one great tool for handling the prospect's deadline tactics is to know your pricing and conditions thoroughly so you won't be enticed into making unrealistic concessions to meet the deadline.

5. The "Take It Or Leave It" Offer. In some types of sales negotiations, things may come to a point where one of the parties tells the other, "That's my final offer." There may be an additional point of emphasis like, "Take it or leave it!" depending upon how animated the negotiations have been. Unlike the budget limitation defense, the buyer has a self-established bogey.

Either the buyer or the salesperson can use this tactic, but unfortunately, the buyer is most often in a better position to do so.

One could assume that this brings the negotiations to a close and the salesperson can either accept the "final offer" or thank the prospect and take off.

Not so! There may still be room for further negotiation.

How to beat the final offer

Here are some suggestions for getting past the "final offer."

a. Pretend you never heard it and continue with the negotiations.

b. Assume that the buyer isn't really serious. Check it out by questions.

c. Review the terms to see if you both agree on what they are. "As I understand it, Mrs. Andrews, you are offering so-and-so. That means we are almost in agreement, doesn't it?"

d. Restate the benefits of accepting your proposal at the price. Emphasize the loss from not buying, the risks in not accepting now.

e. Change the proposal package as in the budget limitations bogey by removing items, changing quantities or qualities, or reducing services to fit the offered price. "I can understand your feelings on price, Mr. Foster. If you will pick up the furniture at our warehouse, I can let you have it at that price. Can you do that?"

f. Isolate the "take-it-or-leave-it" factors and continue negotiations on the rest.

g. If you cannot meet the dollar price, consider offering non-price concessions like added services, extended warranties, training of employees. See Checklist of non-price concessions in Section 9.

h. Give the buyer a chance to back away without losing face if you suspect that it was said in a moment of stress. "I know you don't mean that literally, Mr. Knowland, so let's see what we have here." Take the blame yourself. "I may not have made it clear that we will include a storm door in the price which means a savings of $125. Did you understand that?"

i. If you feel you will have to take the final offer, get a commitment on the sale first. "If I agree to that price, are you willing to sign the order right now?"

j. You may have to reject the final offer, of course. Just be sure you have given these alternatives a try first and end the sales negotiations on a friendly basis. "I'm sorry we couldn't get together, Mrs. Burns. We would have appreciated your business and would have done a good job for you. If you don't mind, I'd like to check back with you in a few weeks to see how things are going. Meanwhile, feel free to contact me for any information you may need."

6. The "I need to get this approved" Tactic. The prospect may lead you to believe that he or she has full authority to make the purchase or make concessions. After you and the buyer have worked out what you think is a firm agreement, the buyer says "I have to take it to the Controller for approval." This tactic gives the buyer another swing at concessions after establishing a new base for negotiations.

This is particularly difficult for the salesperson who has said in advance that he or she has full authority to make concessions. The buyer knows that the salesperson has the authority to agree to whatever else the higher authority asks for.

Check for buying authority

A good defense against this tactic is to establish before starting the negotiation if the other party has full power to approve the purchase. "Do you have authority to approve the contract should we come to an agreement?" If your contact does not have full authority, ask to see the one who does have that authority.

If this doesn't work, at least make clear that you retain equal freedom to reconsider any points that you and the first party agree to when the agreement goes to another for approval.

If you have come to what you thought was a firm agreement with the buyer and the buyer announces the need for another approval, insist on your right to withdraw or modify your own concessions. "I didn't understand that there was to be another party involved, but that's okay. We'll treat our agreement to this point as a rough draft to which neither of us is committed. You check with Mr. Nelson and I'll review it, too, to see if I come up with any changes to suggest."

Another way to treat the situation where the buyer needs to get further approval is to set a time limit for the current agreement without changes. "If Mr. Nelson approves this draft tomorrow, I'll stick by our agreement. Otherwise, each of us will be free to propose any changes."

7. The "Good-guy, Bad-guy" Routine. The good-guy, bad-guy routine has been a favorite interrogation device in the movies for many years. The first interrogator is really rough on the prisoner, threatens all sorts of dire consequences, may even do violence. When the hero doesn't crack, the bad guy takes a break and the good guy takes over. He gives the hero a drink and a cigarette, apologizes for the bad guy but points out that he can't control him. He advises the hero to confess to him while he can get good treatment and before the bad guy gets back.

The good-guy, bad-guy routine has been tried in different kinds of negotiations, too. Here's how it might be used in sales negotiations. One party, the "bad guy," takes a tough stand on price and services. "I won't pay more than $3.16 apiece and only in one gross lots, delivered once a week." His partner, the "good guy," looks embarassed through the whole act. Finally he can't take it anymore and comes in with, "Now look, Sidney. Don't be so unreasonable. Bill, here, has done us a lot of favors. He deserves a decent profit. Let's agree to $3.20 apiece for five gross lots delivered once a month."

The salesperson is supposed to feel so relieved and appreciative of the good guy that he or she will jump at the better offer even though it is still way off a realistic mark.

Sellers use the tactic, too

Needless to say, sellers have used the same tactics against buyers. One twist used in the automobile, real estate and other high ticket fields is for the "good-guy" salesperson to take sides with the customer in wringing out more concessions from the "bad-guy" manager or owner.

Understanding the tactic is the best defense. Know your own base clearly and work from it without being affected by the good-guy, bad-guy routine. "Mr. Ames, I appreciate your consideration. I still feel that my proposal is a fair one, however."

8. Threats. Some customers try to use voiced or implied threats with salespeople in order to get a better deal or some extra consideration. A common threat is to take the firm's business elsewhere unless the salesperson comes around.

If the customer's annual sales are considerable, the customer knows that the threat must get reasonable consideration. In another version, the customer has a problem with product or service and threatens to let his or her friends in the purchasing community know that the salesperson can't be trusted . . . unless the complaint is settled generously.

The threat can be to go over the head of the salesperson to his or her boss or even the president of the firm. How the salesperson responds to the various threats is naturally affected by weighing the consequences against the losses.

While it does nothing for one's morale, salespeople often have to swallow pride to save the business. It helps to be able to call the buyer's bluff, and you do it better with a professional, restrained manner. "Mr. Schuster, I appreciate your business and want to earn it with fair prices and good service. I can't do that, nor can I afford to jeopardize my reputation by responding to threats."

9. The Super-contract Bait. Buyers involved in contracts of considerable size naturally want to get bids from as many responsible sellers as possible. One strategy used that drives salespeople frantic is called the "super-crunch." All the invited suppliers come together for a conference at which time the contract is explained and the size emphasized so that all the suppliers start to drool.

The buyer explains what is desired and gets opinions from each of the representatives on the feasibility of the conditions of the contract. The purpose of the super-crunch is more than just to explain the package, however. It is designed to make the whole group of suppliers uneasy about each other and the possibility that one will cave in to the demands of the buyer when the bid request goes out.

The only defense against the super-crunch is to do your homework with the help of the experts back at the company. Spend time making a complete proposal. Emphasize the services and reputation that go with your proposal. Know your costs, your required margins, and refuse to be suckered into giving everything away.

It's tough to do, and the buyer usually benefits from the super-crunch. That's why it's universally used when the contract is a big one.

10. "What's Your Rock Bottom Price?" A favorite question asked by shrewd buyers of the inexperienced seller goes something like this, "I don't have much time. What is the least you will take for the property?" Of course, the seller can use the same tactic, "What is the most you would pay if you had to?" This tactic, whether used by the buyer or seller, is aimed at getting to a base point on which to negotiate as quickly as possible.

The obvious response to a buyer's rock-bottom request is to avoid giving a quick answer that might leave you no room to negotiate. You have the advantage if you sell products that have relatively stable prices based on quantity and can just turn to your price book and ask, "How many will you need?"

If your pricing is flexible, you can hedge your answer by saying something like, "Well, I think that a fair price is $75,000. Do you agree?" Both you and the buyer will usually understand that this is a negotiable figure but it supplies the starting base.

You don't need to tell all you know

While deliberate deception has no place in professional sales negotiations, good faith negotiation does not insist that the parties must volunteer all they know. Some knowledge is power only as long as it is not known by the other negotiating party. Professional negotiators assume that they must tell the truth when asked a question, or refuse to answer it. Buyers become adept at asking questions that will give the necessary information about the product or service and sales conditions. These questions should be answered by the salesperson correctly.

While salespeople are expected to tell the truth about their product or service, including any minus factors a buyer should know, other types of information need not be volunteered. The salesperson would not be expected to tell a buyer, for example, that the product was moving slowly and that his or her firm was overstocked and open to reasonable price concessions.

Some buyer questions can also be turned aside and still result in an ethical negotiation. "I'm sorry, Mr. Knotts, but I'm not at liberty to give that information."

11. The "What If?" Tactic. A popular tactic used by BOTH salespeople and buyers starts out with the words, "What if . . ." Then follows a hypothetical concession that is not binding on either the buyer or the seller until there is an agreement.

The buyer asks, "What if I agree to take fifteen tons over the next six months. What would the price be then?" The assumption is that the salesperson will reduce the price a bit.

If the salesperson does reduce the price, the buyer still doesn't have to take fifteen tons. It's just a test. But if the new price is agreeable, the buyer can say "It's a deal," and the sales negotiation is completed.

The salesperson might say, "What if we write up the contract so that you don't start payments until the first of the year?" If the buyer says, "Then I'll take it," the salesperson can close if he has the authority, or can say, "Let me check with my manager to see if we can do it." Further discussion on the use of the "What if?" tactic by salespeople is covered in Chapter 4. A comparable tactic also illustrated in Chapter 4 is the "If I . . . will you?" and "If you . . . then I" approach to making concessions.

The value of this tactic for both parties is that there is no commitment to make the concession following the "What if?" but they can assume that the concession will be made if the other party comes up with an acceptable concession in return.

Some buyers use the "what if" tactic to extreme, however, as a way to hack away at the salesperson's proposal. They have a way, too, of recalling previous offers of concessions by the salesperson that were not matched by the buyer at the time but become an add-on nibble after the sale is made. "You said that you would include the carpet, so I expect that to remain." The salesperson can argue rightfully that the concession was withdrawn but will probably give it up to get the sale and get away.

Welcome the "What if" tactic as an evidence of the buyer's willingness to make concessions. But don't give your answer too quickly.

Know your prices and conditions and do your calculations just as you would for any other type of counter offer.

12. Misleading Facts. Despite what we have discussed about the ethics of telling the truth in sales negotiations, one has to assume that some buyers will give incorrect information or at least misleading facts in order to get a better deal.

Unless you know from past experience that you can trust your customer's facts, your best defense is to check any information out that will unduly affect your proposal. People are used to having their credit checked when making a purchase, or having the produce weighed at the supermarket. So as long as you keep personalities out of it and show that checking your facts is the standard routine, the buyer shouldn't take offense at your desire to get the truth.

13. Escalation Tactics or Low-balling. The salesperson assumes that he or she and the prospect have come to a tentative agreement on the terms of the sale. But before the contract is signed, the prospect says something like, "I've checked my figures and find that I can't afford to pay the $2,500 unless you include the installation of the electrical outlets. But if you'll do that, I'll sign right now."

The automobile salesperson fills out a sales contract form and the prospect signs the agreement. The salesperson takes the contract into the manager's office for his signature. The prospect is ready to drive the car off but back comes the salesperson and humbly says, "Gee, I'm so sorry, but I forgot to add in the undercoating charge of $75. So if we increase this amount by just $75, you got yourself a new car."

These are just examples of what are called escalation tactics or "low-balling" in sales negotiations. They can be used by either the buyer or the salesperson as we saw in the examples. Sometimes they are ethical, sometimes not. They are legal as long as the contract has not been signed by both parties.

They are obviously dangerous tactics, too, because the offended party can become emotionally upset and refuse to continue even when the change might not be all that important or if the escalating party drops back to the original agreement.

Salespeople who have to provide a bid or proposal involving a number of items, as in the construction of a building, have the right to escalate the price any time before the contract is signed. This may be done as a correction of an error or a change in the cost of an item. Some salespeople will use the escalation tactics, however, in an attempt to get the prospect to settle for the original amount. The effect intended is that in the face of the salesperson's escalation, the original price seems to be more of a bargain, so the prospect hopefully says, "Hold on, Bill, you said I could have the contract for $25,339 and I'm going to hold you to that."

How to handle escalation tactics

When you understand the use and purpose of the escalation tactics by a buyer, you are in a better position to deal with them. Here are some suggestions:

a. Know your limits for concessions. Don't be pressured into exceeding them just to get the sale.

b. Be willing to say no. The buyer may be bluffing and be just as anxious as you are to close the sale.

c. Get authorized signatures on the contract as soon as possible. Escalation is more difficult after the signatures are on the contract.

d. Be ready to counter escalate. "I'm sorry, I can't agree to the additional outlets. In fact, I've checked the figures and I'll have to add in another $150 for changing the window location."

e. Ask for time to reconsider. "I can understand your wanting to include the furniture in the price, Mr. Forbes. Let me get back to you in a few days after I check out several other prospects for the property." If the prospect was just testing, he may back off and close the sale to avoid losing the property to another buyer.

f. If you have reason to believe that there might be an escalation, ask for assurance against it before signing the contract. "Are we both agreed on the price and terms of the contract?" While not a guarantee against escalation, the additional verbal acknowledgement should help prevent it.

14. The Add-on or Nibble Tactic. After the contract is signed, the customer tries to get you to add something else of value under the guise that he or she assumed it would be included. Negotiators call this tactic "the nibble." It resembles the escalation tactic except that it is used after the sale is completed and the add-on is usually lower in value.

Buyers who use the add-on tactic try it particularly after the salesperson has spent a lot of time and effort to get the initial sale. The buyer assumes that the salesperson will give a small token in desperation to keep the sale. "I'm glad we closed the deal, finally. I assume that we can expect a year's free service on the equipment." The customer knew very well that the guarantee was for just ninety days, but tries the add-on tactic to get nine more months of service free. Other nibbles might be free delivery or training the staff to use the equipment.

Once you are aware that buyers will use the add-on tactic, you can be ready with an appropriate defense. The best defense is to point out that you don't have the authority to make any additional concessions (which is what the tactic really is). If the buyer persists, you might relate a story on how one of the other salespeople in the firm did that three years ago and was fired the next week. Depending on the circumstances and your relations with the buyer, you could assume that he or she is joking and laugh at the request. "Good try, Joe, but you know I can't do that."

If the sale has not been legally closed by having the order signed, the salesperson could consider the add-on request as a reopening of negotiations and try to get a concession from the buyer in return. This is risky, of course, and you could lose the entire sale.

It all boils down to how valuable the add-on is and how you feel about granting it. The main thing is to know it can happen and work out ahead of time how you will handle it.

If you have a customer who uses the add-on tactic repeatedly and if the business is still worth keeping, you might consider holding back some concessions to pay for the add-on or to have some counter chips ready. "Mrs. Thomas, we normally can't afford to install the new casters on your old chairs, but I'll tell what I can do. If you order the five new chair pads we were talking about, I'll have the delivery man put the new casters on your chairs at the same time. Okay?"

How to combat add-on tactics

Here is a list of ways to combat the buyer's add-on tactics. Some we covered before, and you can add more from your own situation and experience.

a. Plead lack of authority to grant the add-on.

b. Show a printed price list that gives the added cost of any extras and specifies the firm's policies.

c. Anticipate the add-on request and determine ahead of time to resist or trade off.

d. Include items that are commonly used as add-ons in the package price. "I suggest that you get the cover for your computer at the same time and I've included it in this proposal." The buyer can decide not to take the cover and asks for a price concession. This gives him or her the same satisfaction as asking later for the add-on of the cover.

e. Use the items included in the package price as trade-off concessions. "Tell you what we can do. If you think you won't need the cover, I can substitute six reams of paper. Would you prefer that?"

f. Assume the customer is joking in your reply. "I know you're just kidding, Jack. You understand that I can't really do that." "Are you trying to get rid of me, Walter? You know the boss would never approve it."

15. The Pick-and-Choose Tactic. Buyers of a large assortment of items like office supplies develop a list of the total requirement of each item for a period of time like six months or a year. Then they ask the available supplier salespeople to submit bids on the total volume of items.

When the bids are in, the buyer finds that some firms will bid lower on some items and higher on others when compared to their competitors. The easiest solution is to accept the lowest total bid even though that salesperson might be higher on some items than other bidders. In most situations of this kind, the cost of time and paperwork for multiple orders, deliveries and payments will be more than the savings in "picking and choosing" the lowest bids for individual items from several suppliers.

Yet there are buyers who feel they must use the "pick-and-choose" strategy to justify their position.

There may be a few items that are used in large enough volume to warrant separate bids, like the paper used in office copiers. In this case, the buyer would pull copier paper from the general list of office supplies and get bids on it separately.

Another variation of the pick and choose strategies is one that Chester Karrass calls "cherry-picking." Here the buyer tries to negotiate several bidders down to the lowest prices offered for each item during the bidding.

One bidder is lowest on machine ribbons in the office supplies example but higher on file folders than at least one other bidder. The buyer tries to get that salesperson to cut the price of file folders to match the lowest bid even though the salesperson with that bid was higher on ribbons. This tactic is ethical but is difficult for salespeople to handle.

How to handle the pick-and-choose buyer

Here are some suggestions for handling the pick-and-choose negotiator.

a. Know your pricing systems thoroughly. Be ready to hold the line. Some salespeople will make mistakes in pricing and live to regret it.

b. Understand your firm's policy on splitting the list of items. There are risks in insisting on all-or-nothing negotiating, but it's better to lose a sale than to take a loss.

c. Be ready to point out the advantages to the buyer of having one supplier for the whole list. Besides the administrative costs of extra paperwork and handling, you may be able to offer special services providing you get the whole order. Some office supply firms, for example, will handle the inventory management of all the office supplies for the customer, relieving a staff member of that chore.

d. Keep on friendly terms with the customer. A satisfied customer is not so apt to trade short price gains for long range fair prices and good service.

e. Think about a modest drop in total bid rather than changing all high items to give the buyer something to win and report to the boss.

16. Switching and Adding Negotiators. One of the tactics used in most forms of negotiation is to change the parties to the negotiation when things get deadlocked or when one party feels that the other has reached the limit on concessions. Usually this tactic favors the new party to the negotiation for several reasons. The change is disconcerting, particularly when one is weary and there is a tendency to want to get the whole thing over with. The new party wipes out any antagonism that might have risen between the original parties that keep them from "giving in" on the terms. The new party tends to ignore concessions made by the one being replaced, yet holds the other negotiator to the terms last offered.

Some firms use the tactic of sending in a department manager or similar higher executive after a subordinate buyer has brought the salesperson to a deadlock. The salesperson is expected to be afraid of losing the sale and to be somewhat in awe of the new executive and to respond to his or her new demands.

The executive may also play the "good-guy" role we discussed earlier. "Good old Bill may have been pushing too hard on this proposition. Let's see where we stand and perhaps I can find a way for us to do business."

Salespeople sometimes put the switch in negotiators to good use, too, particularly in selling high ticket brackets like real estate or autos. The sales manager is brought in to replace the salesperson to try to close the sale. This is done in industrial selling when an important sale bogs down at the initial level.

Even presidents have been known to wind up talking to each other about contracts. Some firms use "closer" salespeople who are brought in when the original salesperson gets into a deadlock. They are usually experienced salespeople with particular skill in closing and who can project the expert image to the prospect.

Men's clothing departments and stores often use the "closer" to help the salespeople get the order.

What to do about a new negotiator

Here are some suggestions for handling the possibility of facing a new party in the sales negotiation.

a. Anticipate that this might happen and determine ahead of time how you will react. That way you won't be surprised and thrown off balance.

b. Expect the new party to go back on previous concessions. It's only fair to withdraw your own concessions if this is done.

c. Consider breaking off the talks until you can meet with the original person if you feel that this is important.

d. Try to close the sale with the new party. He or she may be as anxious to close as you are, even at the present terms.

e. Bear in mind that it might be to your advantage to have the new negotiator if he or she has greater authority over the purchase.

17. The "Let's Split the Difference" Tactic. When negotiators are at an impasse, splitting the difference in half sounds like a fair settlement. We are conditioned to accept the settlement because it provides a sure and easy way out. But it could be a larger concession for the salesperson than for the buyer.

When a buyer offers to split the difference, take time to evaluate what half the difference would be just as you would any other price concession. If the buyer hasn't made any significant concessions so far, splitting the difference might not be a good idea.

Since the buyer is in a concession mood, if you can't agree on the split, offer an alternative. "Well, I can't split the difference but here's what I can do."

18. The Information Clam. Buyers skilled in negotiations try to keep the salesperson from knowing their real needs, interests and priorities. They know the power in negotiations of knowing what the other party wants and their deadlines and limitations. It is not unusual, in fact, for a shrewd buyer to throw the salesperson off by appearing to have an interest in something else rather than in the product or service eventually purchased.

If the prospect has a real desire to own the deluxe Model A business copier, for example, she might encourage the salesperson to make a proposal on the lesser Model B. With the sale of Model B getting nowhere, the prospect says, "Well, I don't know. What kind of a deal would you give me on Model A?" Having invested the time and apparently losing the sale, the salesperson is expected to come up with a better proposition on Model A than would have been the case had the prospect expressed an earlier interest in it.

The best time for the salesperson to get information about the prospect and the needs and desires is before the negotiations start. Once they start, the prospect may be reluctant to give out information that would make him or her vulnerable. Some of this information can be obtained in the prospecting stage as we will find later. Some of it can be gained in the approach stage by asking probing questions as covered in Chapter 7.

19. Intimidation by "Experts". Customers should know their own business well. In many cases, they will know it better than you do. But in your specialty product or service field, chances are that you know as much as anyone in the customer's group and in many cases, much more.

There will be times, however, when the customer or a specialist called into the negotiation session will play an expert's role and attempt to dominate the decisions.

Experts are expected to have an influence on the negotiations wherever their opinions have weight in the decision. Will a product work? What was the past experience? What are future trends? What is the market in the area now? Is the cost worth the investment?

People with less expertise tend to be reluctant to challenge the expert's input.

When faced with an expert customer, or an expert the customer brings into the sales negotiation, welcome the information they bring but don't be so impressed with the credentials that you fail to utilize your own special knowledge, training and experience.

How to negotiate with the "experts"

Here are some suggestions for working with an expert.

a. Don't go on the defensive. Keep your own expertise in product or service in perspective and be ready and willing to make comparisons.

b. Test and evaluate the degree of expertise carefully. Is it relevant to the subject of the sales negotiation? An expert in one field is frequently incompetent in another and yet people tend to be in awe of whatever he or she says.

c. Experts tend to thrive on acceptance as such. Give your full verbal appreciation. "I certainly value your experience, Miss Walters, and I know that you'll recognize the importance of this feature in our device . . ."

d. Don't equate wealth or official position with expertise on whatever the subject of the sales negotiation is. Respect the power of the authority to affect the outcome of the sale in other ways, but don't be reluctant to challenge opinions or facts on the issue that could jeopardize the sale.

e. Take advantage of the authentic expert's contribution as well as his or her ego. Play down your own knowledge in order to get the expert on your side. "I'm glad you're here because I'd like your opinion. People say that this feature could save many manhours of work every month, but I'm not sure I know why. Could you explain its advantage to me in saving time?"

f. Ask questions to get the expert to give the answers you want instead of giving the information yourself. "How would being able to get 30 more copies a minute with this machine affect your getting out your weekly reports, Miss Johnson?" "How do you feel about the safety of your employees who deliver the proceeds of your sales to the bank each day?"

20. Sticks and Stones. Some buyers delight in poking fun at salespeople and making disparaging remarks to them. Psychologists have various explanations for this including the feeling of power it gives the buyer. "Hey, Joe, you look terrible. Aren't sales going too well for you?" "Come on, now. That's the stupidist thing I've heard you salespeople say this week."

We have to assume that this browbeating is aimed as forcing salespeople to feel so inferior that they have to bend to the buyer's demands on the sale.

Humiliation isn't always verbal. Buyers can attack your status as a salesperson by letting other people interrupt your presentation, stop to make phone calls, or continue to read or work while you talk. Every salesperson has horror stories of this type of harrassment to tell.

The best defense against the "sticks and stones" treatment is to realize what is going on and not let it get to you. If the account is worth getting, hang in there. Weigh the abuse against the possible sale.

It may help to let the buyer know you don't appreciate the treatment, but in a businesslike manner. "Mr. Stetson, I've apparently called on you at a bad time. I have some important information you should know about, so can we set another time when it would be more convenient to you? How about Thursday at ten?"

Some buyers like salespeople to fight back, with a smile, of course. It's best not to assume a particular buyer feels this way, however, until you can test him or her out carefully. The main caution, of course, is not to let the abuse affect your decisions on the conditions of the sale. This will defeat the buyer's probable purpose and in itself is a personal victory for you.

21. The Loud and Abusive Buyer. Some buyers have a mean streak as part of their nature. Others use loud and abusive language and manner with the purpose of intimidating the salesperson into granting more concessions faster in order to close the sale and get away. The best approach the salesperson can take with the abusive prospect or customer is to mentally consider that person as someone with a problem rather than an adversary to trade blows with.

You can refuse to go toe-to-toe with such a person without cringing or backing down. Listen him or her out. Use questions to encourage more talking. Often this allows the buyer let off steam and cool down. Lower your voice and talk normally. Continue to make your presentation with confidence. The contrast in behavior usually brings the high person down. At least it has a positive effect on others who may be in on the negotiations. This isn't an easy solution, admittedly. We tend to want to fight back with comparable fury.

If the sale is important, hang in there. If the possible sale isn't worth the hassle with the abusive prospect, thank him or her and leave.

22. The "What's Your Cost Breakdown?" Tactic. Salespeople who regularly make proposals for services involving labor, supplies and equipment like the construction business, landscaping, building interiors or even educational programs, are exposed to the buyer's tactic of asking for a cost breakdown from which the proposal was made. On the surface, this sounds like the buyer is just interested in what the job entails. But if the salesperson gives out that information, the buyer has a good tool for getting a better price.

The breakdown will show where and how much the profit is so the buyer can cut into it. Looking at the cost of various elements, the buyer may decide to get bids on some of them and take away some of the profit.

Except in certain contracts where cost breakdowns are required, such as government jobs, the salesperson does not have to give them to the buyer. If you are asked, just politely refuse. "I'm sorry I can't give you that information, Mr. James. But I can assure you that you will get quality work at a reasonable price."

You can blame it on your estimators if you like. "I'm sorry, I don't have that information. I just have the proposal figures."

23. The Silent Treatment. Silence can be almost as frustrating to a negotiator as emotional outbursts. Spouses whose partners give them the silent treatment will be sympathetic to how this works. It may take longer to get the sale from the silent-treatment prospect than from one who pulls no punches on objections or problems. The only solution to the stone-faced, silent type prospect or customer is to use questions to pry the feelings and opinions out.

24. The Power Play. Some buyers who are aware of their power like to use the veiled threat during negotiations. They are too professional to come right out and say they'll take their business elsewhere if they don't get the lowest price in the area, but they make sure you understand that. "Last year we had to drop a supplier after we found that one of our competitors was buying from them with an additional 5% discount. Of course I know you wouldn't do that to your customers, would you?" "We once got our shipment of parts three days late and of course we cancelled the rest of the order and switched suppliers. I assume that you can guarantee delivery on the specified date."

When pitted against a person with obvious negotiating power, it may be the wise tactic to ask for fairness.

When a person in power feels that his or her power is recognized by the salesperson and is not threatened, being merciful adds to the feeling of importance. "I certainly respect your position, Mr. Sterling, and I only ask that we be given a fair chance to show you that we can do a good job for you at a reasonable price." "I commend you for your loyalty to your present supplier, Miss Thomas. In all fairness, however, why not let us provide a small amount of your cleaning supplies for six months to test out our service?"

MORE DEFENSIVE TACTICS COMING

Good negotiators have guidelines for resisting making concessions and for minimizing the impact of concessions that have to be made. Those that are particularly effective for salespeople are covered in Chapter 4.

You will find additional tactics for defending yourself against the objections, resistance and pressures buyers use to get price concessions in Chapter 9.

A Good Offense is the Best Defense

For the rest of the book we will discuss ways to develop your sales negotiation power, your own negotiation strategies and tactics, and how to combine them with your basic selling skills.

As you gain personal knowledge and experience in negotiation you will collect and develop additional techniques for coping with the professional buyers' negotiation strategies.

With the proper balance of defensive and offensive negotiating skills, both you and your customers will benefit from those increased sales where everyone wins.

3

Developing Your Sales Negotiating Strength

Evaluate the Balance of Power

THE key to the outcome of any negotiation is the balance of power between the parties. Throughout history, the stronger countries militarily have dictated the terms of agreement to weaker ones. The larger and more powerful companies in business have taken over the smaller and weaker ones.

The outcome of wage negotiations has been determined by the degree of economic power each of the parties could bring forth if challenged.

The experts in negotiation strategy emphasize the importance of the parties assessing the elements of strength and weakness each has before going to the negotiating table and then making a judgement on who has the favorable balance. Dr. Chester L. Karrass stresses the importance of the Balance of Power and identifies categories of power negotiators may have in varying degrees. Herb Cohen classifies power as one of the three crucial variables in any negotiation . . . Power, Time and Information.

In preparation for sales negotiation, salespeople have to evaluate the balance of power between them and the prospect or customer.

How much leverage does each party have that could be used to influence the outcome of the sales negotiation? While trying to identify and assess the balance of power in an upcoming sales negotiation, the salesperson has to keep several factors in mind about sales negotiation advantages.

1. The advantage can be real or assumed. If either party assumes the other has an advantage and acts accordingly in the negotiation, it makes no difference whether that advantage is real or not. A prospect may not be aware that a competitor has a lower price for the same item, but if the salesperson assumes that the prospect does know it, the prospect has the power.

2. The advantage is effective only if understood. The prospect may need the salesperson's product because no other one will work satisfactorily, but if the salesperson doesn't realize he has that advantage, he will not exercise it during the negotiation.

3. The advantage is effective only if accepted. Salespeople know that prospects have the power to refuse to buy, but they can still resist making unreasonable concessions in order to get the sale. The salesperson may be aware of the lofty position of a prospect who is the vice-president of the company and still not be awed by him. The prospect may recognize the salesperson's advantage of an impending price increase and still not be willing to overextend the inventory to avoid it.

4. The advantage need not be used to be effective. If one party believes the other could take certain harmful actions, then the ability to take those actions is an advantage in the negotiations whether or not they are actually taken. The salesperson is afraid that a regular customer will stop buying from him unless a concession is made. The advantage of the customer is effective even though the customer may not have threatened to use it.

5. Using your advantage involves risks. Having a certain advantage is fine, but it is not always the best strategy to use it to gain a sale. Salespeople may be able to use the power of persuasion or economic leverage to get a prospect to buy an inferior product, more than is needed, or the wrong product or service. But eventually a dissatisfied customer will jeopardize future business, often causing losses far more extensive than the immediate gain on the sale.

13 TYPES OF STRENGTHS USED IN SALES NEGOTIATION

Both the salesperson and the customer have varying degrees of strength that can help swing the movement and outcome of the negotiation. They each have an advantage in one factor or another, and when these come into a reasonable balance, the sale is made on a win-win basis.

On rare occasions, one of the parties may have so much advantage that the outcome is win-lose, the salesperson or the customer wins most, depending upon who has the greatest advantage and elects to use it.

There is a wide range of specific strengths any one negotiator may have that will have an effect on the outcome of any negotiation if they are utilized and accepted by the opposing party.

The authors of texts on general negotiation identify and describe many of these special sources of strength and power. Salespeople should be aware of the availability of these strengths in either their own negotiating position or in that of the buyer. Such an understanding and appraisal will help in preparing for and planning the sales negotiation.

Let's identify and examine some of the strengths most apt to be available to one or both of the parties in a sales negotiation.

1. Knowledge is Power. Many schools use as their motto, "Knowledge is Power," from the works of Sir Francis Bacon. Knowledge about the product or service, its application to the prospect's needs or problems or wants, are sources of strength for the salesperson in the negotiation.

Additional elements of knowledge for the salesperson include competitive products, laws and regulations, and information about the prospect or customer. The prospect has negotiating strength through knowing his or her own needs, problems and desires, a knowledge of competitive products and prices, goals and objectives of the prospect's firm, and limits to which the buyer will go in the various terms to be negotiated.

The prospects also have negotiating strength if they have knowledge of the salesperson's costs, organization, products or services, what was done for past customers, pressures to make a sale and the salesperson's personal needs and desires. It is obviously a good strategy for salespeople to keep any facts from becoming known that would give the buyer an advantage.

The chapters which follow give suggestions for assembling the knowledge that will give you added negotiating power.

2. Expertise in the Product Field. Salespeople with regular customers are able to establish themselves as experts in their product field and become advisers and consultants to their customers on product selection and use. This power of expertise is very valuable in sales negotiations and will continue as long as the advice proves right and is not abused. The customers are willing to accept the salesperson's recommendations in the purchase of the product or service and are often willing to pay a premium for the product in order to get the consulting service as part of the package.

Salespeople calling on prospects rather than customers have to establish their credibility as advisers early in the session in order to gain this added strength in the sales negotiation. The total negotiating strength can come from the expertise of the salesperson, the company's experience and reputation, and the past performance of the product or service for other customers.

Elements of the sales presentation should include items that help establish the power of expertise, like testimonials, cases, pictures, research studies, charts and other evidence of capability to solve problems similar to those of the prospect. For example, the salesperson might say, "After I studied the procedure of the Atlas Company, we installed this equipment and were able to cut their operating costs 17%."

This kind of reference will help the salesperson get permission to survey the prospect's procedures.

3. Competitive advantages. Competition, or the lack of it, can provide a balance of power for either the salesperson or the buyer. When prospects or customers have several sources available for similar products or services, they have the balance of power in negotiating the price and other terms.

When the salesperson has the only product that will provide a desired benefit, or the one best suited for the job, he or she has the balance of competitive power.

The professional salesperson is careful to know as much about the competition as possible but avoids mentioning competitors to the prospect.

The professional buyer makes it part of the job to know as much about the various sources of the products and services used as possible. Both are aware that such knowledge is power in the sales negotiation.

The whole energy of a firm's production and marketing activity is devoted to improving the competitive power of their salespeople in sales negotiation with prospects and customers.

Meanwhile, the purchasing departments of the same firms are studying ways to investigate and exploit the many elements of competition in order to get the best possible return on their purchasing investment. When the sale is made, the many factors of competition have come into balance for both parties in the sales negotiation.

4. Persuasive Skills. Most sales are made on appeals to emotions rather than pure logic. That's why salespeople are trained to recognize a prospect's buying motives and to appeal to them by emphasizing the features and benefits that best match those appeals. The salesperson's persuasive expertise helps the prospect decide to buy the product or service when the benefits of ownership outweigh the pain of parting with the money. Salespeople with persuasive skills come out of sales negotiations with the order more often than competitors with similar products but lacking the same level of ability to persuade or convince the prospect.

Persuasive power is not limited to salespeople in sales negotiation, however. Persuasion works just as well for the buyer as it does for the seller. Professional buyers understand that salespeople can be motivated to make concessions by appeals to emotions as well as logic, too. One such buyer might ask, "Would it be helpful to your sales record, George, if we placed this order before the end of December?"

5. Reward and Punishment. Whoever has the power to reward or punish the opponent has an advantage in sales negotiation. Usually there is a balance of reward power in the buy-sell situation. The salesperson has a product or service that can reward the buyer with a benefit. The buyer can agree to buy and pay for the product or service and thus reward the salesperson with income and prestige of success. In a win-win sales negotiation, both parties have the ability and the willingness to give rewards worthy of a successful settlement.

The party with the power to inflict any kind of punishment upon the other will have leverage in the negotiation. Every prospect has the power of punishment in that he or she can refuse to buy. The salesperson has punishment power when in the position of being able to withhold a product or service that the customer wants and which is not readily available from another source. While this advantage is not often available to salespeople in this competitive world, refusing to sell the product unless the prospect meets certain terms is an example of a salesperson's ability to punish.

In periods of shortages when products are rationed, salespeople find themselves in the position of having to punish some customers and reward others. While this may seem like an ideal situation, bear in mind that a salesperson's income usually suffers, too, when there is a shortage of products to sell.

There are other forms of punishment possible by both sides of the sales negotiation. Each may go over the head of the other to higher authority if the negotiation doesn't succeed at their level.

The buyer can threaten to remove the salesperson or the firm from the bidding list, or to stop buying other products from the same company. The punishment may also be psychological such as forcing delays that increase tension and anxiety.

6. The Advantage of Legitimacy. Laws, regulations, rules, positions of authority, tradition, public pressure, respect of others, are forms of legitimacy that can give an advantage to either party in sales negotiation. There are laws and regulations regarding uniform pricing that restrain a salesperson from giving a better price to one customer, and give the salesperson a legitimate reason for refusing to go lower.

The company's printed prices, quantity discounts and terms of sale are forms of legitimacy that give the salesperson added power. As buyers, we read the printed price tag on an appliance and assume it's not negotiable when in fact it might be.

When the prospect asks, "What would it cost if I bought a hundred instead of fifty?" it's a big advantage to have a printed discount schedule to quote from. The prospect assumes there's no chance of reducing the printed figure.

Purchasing executives may set up rules regarding the days and times when they will see salespeople. Yet professional salespeople know they will see salespeople when they are convinced that it is to their advantage to do so. A buyer may point to an internal report and say, "As you can see, we have budgeted only $10,000 for new equipment, so there's no point in discussing your proposal that costs $15,000." The printed budget is a form of legitimacy.

Salespeople most often use the advantage of legitimacy through printed sales contracts and order forms. These are obviously written with the company's interest in mind. When the salesperson says, "This is our standard contract, please sign where I have placed the X," the typical buyer assumes that there's no point in reading the terms because, after all, it is the standard printed contract and no deviations would be permitted. This is not so, of course, but such forms provide the advantage of legitimacy unless challenged. If you work for an ethical company, the sales contract is undoubtedly fair to the buyer with no legal terms or fine print designed to take advantage of the buyer. Use the printed forms to save time and arguments where you can, knowing that they spell out the conditions satisfactory to your company. But be ready to negotiate changes in the wording with customers who are aware of their rights to make changes.

Experts on negotiation point out the need for challenging any form of supposed legitimacy which is brought into the negotiation by the opposing party. Even rules that were "chiseled in stone" have been known to be changed when challenged by the right logic and emotions.

Purchasing agents will see salespeople at times other than the posted hours. Salespeople have succeeded in making sales that exceed a customer's printed budget after they demonstrated the benefits of investing the additional money.

Take advantage of legitimacy when it is on your side. But be prepared to challenge any legitimacy when it stands in your way during the sales negotiation.

7. History of Past Performance. Both the salesperson and the potential buyer must feel assured that the other party will live up to the commitments made during the sales negotiation. The prospect wants to believe that the salesperson and his or her firm will deliver the product and service that was agreed upon. The salesperson wants to believe that the customer will pay for the product or service on the terms in the agreement and will not play tricks to get further concessions or get out of agreements after the sale is made.

The salesperson who can show evidence of satisfied customers and the firm's history of living up to warranties and adjusting customer complaints, has an advantage over suppliers who lack such a reputation.

Friendships and loyalties built up by salespeople and customers over a period of time through satisfactory performance make it easier for both parties to get agreement during the sale negotiation.

Salespeople and professional buyers who are loyal to their respective companies tend to respect that loyalty in each other and negotiate more effectively.

8. Investment of Time and Effort. Selling and intelligent buying call for the investment of reasonable time and effort. Those salespeople who are willing to take the time and effort to plan for the sales negotiation, to collect the knowledge, to develop the skills required, to do the paperwork and preparation chores, will have the advantage over less prepared competitors in sales negotiations.

The potential buyer who is willing to take the time and effort to check on the availability of the product or service, competitive sources, the market's going prices and fringe benefits available, will have an advantage in the sales negotiations.

People who are lazy or lack patience give up important negotiation power to others willing to work and wait out solutions to problems.

The investment in time and effort provides a special advantage that should be recognized. After we have invested considerable time and effort in anything, we hate to give up on it without a struggle.

Salespeople who spend considerable time trying to land a new customer tend to be more likely to make concessions to salvage the sale. Professional buyers are aware of this unique characteristic of time investment and try to wear the salesperson down to concessions to salvage the investment. Salespeople need to be alert to this possibility and not "give the store away" just to justify the time and effort spent on getting the sale.

Buyers can also be influenced by the amount of time and effort they have invested in finding just the right product or service that will satisfy their needs. When a salesperson comes along with just the right solution, the tendency is to buy it without the usual negotiation. It is naturally a favorable balance of power for the salesperson to know when this is the situation.

9. Time Pressures. "Time is Money" is the title of a seminar we produced on time management for salespeople. How salespeople manage their time directly affects their sales and income.

For buyers, getting something that is needed sooner can save money and make more profits. Getting the right proposal in before a critical date can result in a sale for a salesperson. Getting it there late can lose the sale.

So, time pressures can give an advantage to either party in the sales negotiation. Whichever party is hampered by time limits gives the other party extra negotiating power. The approaching date when contracts will be opened gives added pressure for the salesperson to make the best possible proposal. A dwindling inventory of needed supplies forces the buyer to be more receptive to the salesperson who can get the order delivered before the current supply runs out. That's why firms are careful to have a good system of inventory management with effective lead time for ordering and early-warning signals. They know that time pressures can increase the price they will have to pay for inventory replenishment.

10. Precedent. Salespeople often come up against a prospect who doesn't want to make a change because, "We've always done it this way and don't want to change now," or, "We've bought from Wiggins for twenty years and see no reason for changing now."

People resist making changes, so precedent can be a strong factor when facing a prospect for the first time in a sales negotiation, or when trying to get a present customer to make some changes in adding new lines or new furniture. The salesperson has to present acceptable reasons why it will be to the advantage of the customer to accept his or her proposal. The benefits will have to outweigh the desire for leaving things as they are.

Salespeople sometimes have the advantage of precedent in sales negotiations when their product is widely used by others or when a procedure has worked well over a period of time. Obviously, the salesperson should be ready to exploit this advantage by showing proof of previous successes through testimonials, cases, pictures, or reports.

11. Negotiating Tenacity. Sales negotiations are often won by one side simply because that person or group hung in there longer, tried harder, refused to give up against the odds. There are many instances given in books on selling and by experts in the field where a sale was finally made by the salesperson who called more often, or made more presentations than the competitors. It wasn't a matter of wearing the prospect out, although that could be a factor. It was usually a case of where the salesperson finally found the right incentive to buy and the situation or mood was just right for the prospect to say yes.

It happens in love stories and it happens in sales negotiations every day.

There obviously has to be a distinction between being persistent or tenacious and becoming a nuisance to be avoided by the prospect. Salespeople with tenacity or persistence seldom take the first few "no's" at their face value. They try to avoid an argument, of course, but they keep coming back to the proposition, perhaps from another angle or with some modifications including concessions from both sides.

The key to workable tenacity is the ability of the salesperson to offer a fresh approach to the prospect, another suggestion of a benefit from buying the product or service. The prospect is generally open to new ideas but might object to the continuous repetition of the same old arguments.

Professional buyers also recognize the value of tenacity. They know they can wear some salespeople down and get more concessions simply by continually raising questions and objections and stalling in making a buying decision. That's why salespeople are trained in the strategies of handling resistance and objections and in ways to close the sale.

12. Patience. Throughout history, patience has been shown to be a powerful force in successful negotiations for the side willing to use it. Peace and labor negotiations have shown that the party who gets too hasty to settle usually comes off on the short end of negotiations.

Patience is a powerful tactic in sales negotiations when it can be used. Time and patience are partners, of course, and unfortunately many sales negotiations are carried on under time pressures. Even within a time frame of as little as a half-hour, patience to outwait the other party or to try another suggestion or concession could be the tactic that swings the ultimate sale.

Both the buyer and the salesperson can gain from using patience. It gives each more opportunity to evaluate the benefits and the costs of the product or service. It allows each to test the other's strengths and weaknesses so they can be more properly negotiated. Patience gives time to try new alternatives that might change the attitudes.

Salespeople must understand the value of patience in the successful conclusion of sales negotiations and avoid writing off the quick session as a failure too soon. If time restraints become a factor, try extending the negotiations to another time. Make another appointment. Don't give up too soon!

13. Negotiating Skill. Just as persuasive skills are added power for the salesperson, so are the skills in negotiation strategies and tactics. Many sales are won (when all other factors are comparable) through the extra negotiating skill a salesperson has developed.

That's why this book came about, and all the ideas and suggestions given here are aimed at increasing the salesperson's negotiating skills along with the basic professional selling skills.

The buyer may also have had negotiation skill training, or may be skilled simply through experience, trial and error. But when salespeople are also skillful in negotiation strategy, they are able to recognize the tactics the buyer is using and can take the steps necessary to cope with them.

When both parties to the sales negotiation are skilled in negotiation strategies, the effect is not one of competitiveness but rather one of making the sales negotiation go much smoother and come to a satisfactory conclusion sooner. The mutual respect of the salesperson and the buyer tends to bring them together.

PREPARE TO NEGOTIATE FROM STRENGTH

Professional salespeople have always considered their personal, company and competitor strengths when planning and developing their sales calls and presentations. So it is easy for them to consider these same strengths as factors in sales negotiation. With the awareness of the value of negotiation skills, however, these strengths can be integrated with predetermined negotiating strategies to provide a more effective approach, presentation and close.

With the added awareness of the possible negotiating power and skills the buyers could have, the salesperson can be better prepared to cope with the buyer's tactics such as were described in Chapter 2.

In the Chapters which follow, you will find many ideas and suggestions that will help you acquire and take advantage of your own strengths during the sales negotiation. You will also find help in coping with the advantages your prospects and customers may enjoy.

As you study these Chapters, review from time to time the factors we have discussed here which can give both you and your prospect or customer advantages in varying degrees. Approach each Chapter with the special objective of collecting strategies and tactics for building your power base for sales negotiations and for dealing with the strengths of your prospects and customers.

4

Sales Negotiation Strategies and Tactics

Good Selling Strategies Not Enough

PROFESSIONAL salespeople have developed a personal base of selling strategies and tactics which they call into use when planning or involved in a sales situation. They work well for most sales negotiation situations, too.

But there are certain strategies and tactics used by professional negotiators that can be added by salespeople to their existing techniques to make more sure that the outcome of their sales negotiations will be in their favor.

Training in selling strategies usually follows a logical sequence of actions sometimes referred to as the "steps in the sale." The salesperson develops a background of product knowledge, then looks for a qualified prospect. After selecting a prospect, the salesperson follows a strategy of planning for the presentation, making the presentation, handling resistance and finally closing the sale.

No "Steps" In Negotiating Strategies

Sales negotiation strategies and tactics do not follow a logical outline as easily. Most of them, while involving some pre-planning, are used when face to face with the prospect or customer. In selling, this is basically during the sales presentation phase where the salesperson makes the proposal, handles resistance and convinces the prospect to buy.

In this chapter, we will review the strategies and tactics used by negotiators in any field, but which are especially appropriate for use by salespeople in sales negotiation.

We will not try to follow any artificial "steps to sales negotiation". Instead, we will take the techniques one by one in no particular order of relative importance. We will keep related strategies and the tactics involved together as much as practical, however.

STRATEGIES VS TACTICS

The dictionary clearly differentiates between the terms, strategy and tactics. In actual negotiations, however, it is sometimes difficult to tell whether a move is part of a strategy or a tactic. The technical distinction is not important so long as the strategies and tactics are understood.

However, we will consider something as strategy if it is a technique used in the overall process of sales negotiation. We will consider tactics as lesser actions required to implement and carry out the strategy.

In Part II, starting with Chapter 5, we will combine the best strategies of selling and negotiation. While much of the discussion will be in the area of basic selling skills professionals use, the strategies of negotiation have been added to strengthen the salesperson's total approach to the usual sales negotiation situations.

Be Ready to Negotiate

Be prepared with all the strength and advantages you can collect before you enter sales negotiation. From your study of Chapter 3, you have probably found that you have more leverage than you realized that you can use to favor your side of the negotiation.

Know as much about the prospect as possible, the needs, desires, problems, present conditions, present suppliers, personal preferences, authority to buy, and whatever other information is available or worth finding that will be helpful. Be sure of your initial proposal.

When negotiating in other fields, each party tries to make the other one make the first offer. In sales negotiation, however, salespeople usually have to make the first offer. Be especially sure of your pricing structure and sales conditions so you won't make a serious mistake or be maneuvered into a bad concession. Know where your limits are as well as what you may be able to concede later. Have your initial asking price and conditions well thought out.

Know where your bottom line is.

Evaluate the Alternatives

As a salesperson, you will become involved in some form of negotiation during every sale. In those instances where it becomes apparent that more intense negotiation will be necessary to land the sale, you will have to determine whether or not you really want to work that hard at getting the sale.

Will the time and effort you spend on the negotiations be worth it in present or future sales? Will you be personally comfortable in negotiating?

Feel free to pick and choose the situations in which you are willing to get into heavier negotiations. When you do decide to go with it, don't allow yourself to be intimidated by the prospects and customers who like to create a win-lose game with salespeople.

The basic purpose of any negotiation is to produce something better than you can get without negotiation. Before going into the negotiation, it is well to determine what that alternative would be. It becomes your standard against which any propositions offered during the negotiation can be measured.

In sales negotiation, you go into the activity to get a sale or to get agreements that will eventually result in a sale. What would happen if you didn't make the sale? The world wouldn't fall down around you. You might lose a little income but you could get that back on the next sale. If you happen to be selling a special article like an antique chest, if you don't negotiate this sale, there's another opportunity perhaps tomorrow. On the other hand, this sale might be very important for a number of reasons, unlike other possible sales to other prospects.

Whatever the alternative is to a successful sales negotiation, it is sort of a bottom line against which you measure your actions during the negotiation.

If the sale is critical, you may weigh your concessions more carefully, give more to get the sale.

If the sale is routine, you will probably be more firm in your concessions, spending less time with a reluctant prospect.

Thinking through your alternatives before the negotiation gives you the opportunity to answer this statement, "If I don't get what I want in this negotiation, I can always . . ."

Obviously, the more sure you are that your alternatives are secure, the more effective your bottom line will be based on those alternatives. "If he doesn't give me at least $500 for this car, I can always sell it for that at the City Used Car Sales." "If I can't sell it at cost, I can always give it to charity and take a tax deduction."

Check the Authority of Negotiating Parties

An important rule in selling is to get to the person who has the authority to buy. Many people in a home or firm can say "No, we don't need any." But only one or a few persons have the authority to make the buying decision if they like your proposal.

Make sure that you're negotiating with the right person. Don't waste time negotiating with a person who does not have the authority to buy. This doesn't mean that you shouldn't talk with others who can influence the sale, of course. Just don't get down to the negotiating details until you face the person who can authorize the sale.

The Limited Authority Tactic

Sales negotiators may have authority to buy or sell, but only up to a point. Actually this can be an advantage to the party claiming the lack of authority.

As mentioned in Chapter 2, the buyer uses the lack of authority tactic as an excuse for not paying a higher price. But the lack of authority tactic can be used by the salesperson as well. In fact, it may be important for the salesperson not to have full authority to speak for his or her firm.

There sometimes comes a spot in the negotiations where the salesperson should be able to say honestly, "I'm sorry, Mr. Stanton, but I don't have the authority to do that." These can be areas like giving credit, giving a better price, taking back merchandise, or absorbing some charges. The lack of authority takes the salesperson off the hook and allows the negotiations to proceed without malice between the parties. This is one of the reasons top officials seldom get into sales negotiations.

When customers know a salesperson has the authority to grant certain concessions, it is difficult to take a stand against granting them. So the firm grants limited authority to the salespeople which acts as a safety valve against emotional reactions and gives the salesperson a buffer zone against unrealistic demands.

Buyers may have restrictions on their authority to go beyond a budget figure or a total amount of purchase. They may not have authority to buy certain products or services. It may be to their advantage to plead lack of authority when the negotiations reach a certain point. In Section 2 we suggested ways the salesperson can cope with this possibility.

Use limited authority to get an offer

In some instances, the salesperson can use limited authority as a strategy to move the negotiations off dead center and to get the prospect to make an offer. Automobile and real estate salespeople use this strategy effectively.

Without going into detail on the tactics involved or evaluating the ethics sometimes fractured, the procedure is roughly this. When the prospect balks at the figure given, the salesperson pleads lack of authority to make further concessions but offers to take any proposal the prospect makes to higher authority. The contract is filled out on the prospect's terms and he or she signs it. The salesperson takes it to whatever higher authority is available, usually the sales manager. In real estate sales, the salesperson takes the offer to the owner.

Skeptics argue about what goes on in the higher authority's office, but the negotiating procedure is that the salesperson returns with the verdict. It may be, "Congratulations, Mr. Jones, you've just bought yourself a fine car." Or there may be more nibbles like, "Boy, we almost made it. The boss says that if you'll pay for the undercoating and take standard wheel covers, you have a deal. Okay?" Now the negotiation is back in the prospect's court and he can agree, make another offer, or walk out.

An important key in this tactic is that the salesperson takes the position on the side of the prospect "against" the higher authority. "Let's write down your offer, and I'll do my best to get it through for you."

This strategy works just as well for the buyer when used in sales negotiations. The buyer says, "I don't have the authority to pay more, but if you make a proposal, I'd be glad to take it in to the vice president and see what WE can do." If the prospect doesn't suggest it, the salesperson can. "I can understand your position, Mr. Forbes. Let me write out a proposal to take to your vice president and I'm sure WE can work this out together."

18 IMPORTANT CONCESSION STRATEGIES

A general rule in negotiation is "Avoid making the first concession." Studies on general negotiation results have shown that those who make the first concession tend to be the eventual losers. Obviously any locked negotiation wouldn't get anywhere until one or the other party makes a concession or an alternative suggestion. We'll assume that you'll hold to your initial proposal as long as you can, going back over the features and benefits and re-selling. But part of your planning has to be what to do when you get into a bind with the prospect and it's either walk out or make a concession.

There are a wide variety of strategies and tactics used by skilled government and business negotiators in making concessions. Let's look at some that salespeople can use to advantage during sales negotiations.

1. *Start your negotiations with your highest expectations in price and conditions.* That way you'll have room to compromise with reasonable concessions. Make it high but realistic.

Assume that the prospect is doing the same thing until you can do some testing.

2. *Avoid making the first major concession.* It gives the appearance that you are too eager to reduce the price. You can be the first to concede on a minor issue, however. This shows the buyer that you are willing to compromise and could start the bargaining.

If you are first on a minor concession, it could encourage the buyer to make the first major concession.

3. *Don't assume that you have to match the customer's concessions one to one.* Instead, weigh the value of your concession against the total value of the prospect's concessions.

Don't fall into the trap of thinking, "She gave one so now I should give one." Hold on.

4. *Don't give a concession away for nothing.* Instead, try to trade one concession for another. "I think I can reduce the price 2% if you can pick it up at our warehouse. Is that possible?"

The best time to get a concession is when you are offering one.

5. *Make sure the customer understands the value of the concession.* He or she should recognize and assign a trading value to each concession. "If I can get a reduction of half a cent per unit, this would mean a savings of about $337 on your total order. How does that sound to you?"

6. *Make concessions in small amounts.* Studies show that negotiation losers tend to give away too much in each concession. Too large a concession tends to tell the prospect that there's a lot more to be trimmed if he will just hold out. Small concessions encourage the buyers to reciprocate. Three, one percent concessions can be as effective as one, five percent concession.

Don't concede too grudgingly, but express a little pain as you do it. Make at least the appearance of carefully weighing the cost. Use a calculator, do some figuring, give thoughtful contemplation before agreeing to the concession. Make each subsequent concession smaller and smaller to show that you are nearing your limit.

Compare these two scenarios for their effect on the prospect's future negotiation strategy. Salesman A smiles, gestures with his hand and says, "No problem. I can give you another 5% off that price." Salesman B, facing another prospect, frowns at the prospect's rejection of the price, then with a look of concern says, "Hmmm. Give me a minute while I check something here." He looks at some charts, uses his pocket calculator, writes down some figures and studies them for a moment before saying, "I tell you what. I think I can get them to take off as much as 1 1/2% if I can convince them that you will buy a hundred cases over the next year. Do you think that's possible?"

There's no proof that either salesperson will get a sale or that B will end up with a better deal, of course. But if you were the average prospect, would you feel that there was more price cutting available through negotiation with Salesman A? On the other hand, would you feel that you had pretty well hit bottom with Salesman B?

7. *Don't jump at the prospect's first concession unless it is to accept your offer.* The odds are in your favor that the prospect will go higher. Besides, you wouldn't want to hurt the prospect's pride by thinking he or she made a mistake by offering too much.

A good rule in negotiations is, "Say no once more before saying yes." You may have to reconsider, but that's better than giving in too much.

8. *Don't advertise your willingness to make concessions.* How would you react as a prospect if the salesperson's opening statement was, "Well, our price is $350, but I'm willing to give you up to a 20% discount." Where would your negotiations start?

9. *Don't jump at the "Let's split the difference" offer.* Splitting the difference sounds like a fair solution on the surface. But it could mean giving away too much for one of the negotiators. Before you agree, do some calculations to see how half of the difference fits into your willingness to negotiate.

If the buyer hasn't made any significant concessions up to now, splitting the difference between you might not be reasonable. If you decide to refuse the split, offer another method at the same time while the buyer is in a concession mood. "No, I can't split the difference, but here's what I can do . . ."

10. *Handle the ridiculous offer with care.* There is a great human temptation for a salesperson to quit the negotiation cold and walk out when a buyer makes a ridiculous offer. It's an insult to your intelligence and indicates lack of respect for all the work you put into the proposal, right? But if the sale is worth a little more time, consider the offer as just another buyer tactic as mentioned in Chapter 2. Keep cool and polite. The buyer probably knows the offer is ridiculous but feels it's worth a try to sound you out.

Some salespeople pass the offer off as a joke, like, "I know you're not serious, Mr. Forbes. Let's review your needs and our proposal again to see how they match up." If the prospect is really serious, keep the door open for reconsideration or future business. "We'd sure like to do business with you, Miss Jacobs, but we're obviously too far apart at the moment. I'd appreciate it if you give the proposal some more thought at your leisure and I'll call you next Thursday to see if there are some changes we could discuss."

11. *Keep track of your concessions.* Be ready to remind the prospect that you have made three concessions to his two and now he owes you one. Even though you know you don't have to match concessions by number, it's still a good bargaining point to try.

12. *Be prepared to withdraw any concession you made before the final sale.* If you earlier said you would be willing to absorb the delivery charges, feel free to withdraw that offer. "Well, I think we could go along with your offer but you would have to pick up the delivery charge, okay?"

Concessions are just bargaining chips. They can be put in and withdrawn until the sale is over.

13. *Understand all the requirements before you start making concessions.* Get all of the prospect's demands out on the table before you start making any concessions in price, quality or performance.

Your concession should be a result of appraising the whole package. If you're aware of an expense item, for example, you can weigh it against the amount of your concession.

14. *Don't assume that the prospect will understand the benefits of your concession.* Emphasize the benefits in the form of cost savings, better quality, time savings, even personal prestige. "I can do this. I'll give you the lower ten gross price for the total order and let you select as many different items as you like to add up to ten gross. That way you can give your customers a wider choice with a smaller initial investment. How does that sound?"

15. *Be willing to admit mistakes and make corrections.* If you made a mistake in calculations or overlooked an important factor that would affect the outcome from negotiations, don't be embarassed to straighten it out before the sale is completed.

Most professional buyers will empathize with an error and go along with it, starting the negotiations over where the error was made. Even after a contract is signed and legally enforceable, adjustments can often be made in the interest of fairness.

16. *Before making a concession, get the commitment to buy from the prospect.* "Suppose we did substitute Grade A material for standard grade. Are you ready to sign the order?"

17. *Don't overevaluate your desire to be liked when making concessions.* Salespeople basically like people and want people to like them. That's a good attitude to live by. But there comes a time in sales negotiation where the desire to be liked by the customer must be evaluated against dollars and cents.

18. *When you start negotiations with a prospect, free yourself from the bonds of your past experiences.* Experiences with similar buyers or even with the immediate prospect. Increase your expectations on the outcome of the sale. Don't assume that the same kind of concessions will be necessary. Things may have changed since you last tried to make a sale.

More Ideas on Concessions Coming

In Part II, we will discuss selling techniques combined with negotiating strategies. There you will find more specific ideas and suggestions you can use to improve your position in sales negotiations. In Chapter 9 you will find more ideas on making and resisting concessions.

Invest in Bottom-Line Insurance

Salespeople can take a hint from professional negotiators and insulate themselves from making a decision during the sales negotiation that they would later regret. This is known as establishing the "bottom line" before going into the negotiation. Both parties to the negotiation should take out this insurance.

The bottom line for the seller is the lowest amount in money and alternatives that will be acceptable. For the buyer, it is the largest amount that would be acceptable. With a bottom line established, it is easier to resist the pressures and temptations of the moment. It may save you from making a decision on impulse you will regret later.

Establishing a bottom line, while providing protection, has some drawbacks as well. It limits the ability to benefit from evidence learned during the negotiations. It also tends to inhibit imagination in coming up with alternative solutions. A bottom line of $50,000 given to a broker for selling a property, for example, could rule out other considerations like an all cash purchase, a delayed settlement or rental with option to purchase.

The salesperson should set the bottom line realistically from the facts and knowledge. If determined arbitrarily, and adhered to without reflection during the negotiation, it could be detrimental in getting the sale.

When the salesperson realizes that a prospect is holding to a bottom line figure, he or she should be ready with good reasons for breaching the arbitrary figure. "I understand why you would want to set a fair bottom line amount, Mr. Briggs. But I'd like to point out the benefits of going a little higher on this occasion."

Use Deadlines to Stimulate Action

Time pressures can offer advantages to either party in negotiations as we pointed out earlier. Deadlines are evidence of that power.

Whoever has control of the deadline has added leverage to get favorable concessions whether it is the salesperson or the buyer. The key is the importance the opposite party assigns the deadline figure.

In general, salespeople should be somewhat skeptical of deadlines imposed by a buyer unless there is good evidence that it is real. You can probably believe a buyer who says, "We're going to review the proposals and place the order next Monday morning." But even in this case, a salesperson with a very good reason for asking for a delay, like a new product availability, has a good chance of stretching the deadline.

There is a risk, of course, but the moral is not to be panicked into unrealistic concessions by a buyer's stated deadlines. We discussed ways to deal with buyer deadlines in Chapter 2, so let's see how salespeople can use deadline strategy to their advantage.

Sometimes the deadlines are self-imposed by the salesperson or imposed by the salesperson's organization. The sales contest ends on the 31st and this sale would surely help you win. Things haven't been going too well and this sale would look good on your monthly report. Your company insists on four weeks for delivery and the buyer wants the merchandise in two weeks. These kinds of deadlines should be evaluated before making concessions or giving up on the sales negotiation.

If the deadline is your own problem, try not to reveal it to the prospect. As time closes in, evaluate the deadline, weighing it against making more concessions, going beyond the deadline, or calling the negotiations into a deadlock . . . for now.

Be alert, too, for changes in the attitude of the prospect as the negotiations appear to be coming to the end. Take the initiative to probe for a new willingness to make a trade-off.

Use Deadlines to Close the Sale

Salespeople can use deadlines of various kinds to stimulate a reluctant prospect or customer to take action now instead of later. . . or at all!

Here are some examples of deadlines salespeople use for leverage. You will be able to add more from your own experience in selling your product or service. Keep them in mind so they can be used during the sales negotiation when a favorable buying decision is needed.

1. "Our prices go up 5% on the first of the month."
2. "This is a special package offer that expires next week."
3. "When these are gone, they won't be restocked."
4. "When I checked last, there were just four chairs of that style left. Let me call and see if they're still available."
5. "If you don't take these, it will take six weeks to get another order in."
6. "Unless I get your approval today, I can't meet your delivery date."

7. "I've been allowed to offer this lower price for just ten days. After that it will go up to $11.40 apiece."

8. "Our next delivery to your area is Thursday morning. If you give me your order today, I'll make sure it's on that truck."

9. "It will take seven weeks to get your special order through production. I suggest that you use our Model 125 which is very similar and is immediately available."

More ideas for closing the sales negotiation, including the use of deadlines as an Inducement Close, are found in Chapter 10.

Minimize the Stress of Deadlines

Competent negotiators know the stress involved with deadlines as well as their contribution to negotiations. Stress tends to force agreement by one or both parties to the sales negotiation before the time deadline is reached.

Salespeople are used to losing sales, so the professionals have less problem with stress resulting from approaching deadlines in sales negotiations. But there has to be some stress for any salesperson when a big order hinges on bringing the negotiations to a successful close within the deadline.

There are a number of good books on stress and ways to handle it. A classic is Psycho-Cybernetics by Maxwell Maltz that has been credited with changing the lives of many people who were able to adjust and modify their stressful life style. If you apply the logic in the book, you would avoid some of the stress in sales negotiations by saying to yourself, "Hey, what's the worst that could happen? I lose the sale. But that's happened before and I'm still alive. Besides, I may get another crack at the prospect or even find a better one."

You can't ignore some deadlines, of course, and you should give the important ones your best shot. But you can handle them better when you consider them part of the selling profession and not a life-threatening event. Besides, the deadline may be negotiable, too, if you can come up with a good reason for extending it!

Deadlines have a way of encouraging agreement, so keep your stress level normal and be patient. Remember that the prospect usually has a deadline problem, too, even though he or she may be good at keeping the fact under cover. Be alert for a favorable moment to get a conclusion, a suggestion, a minor concession or additional offer. If you have nothing more you can do, just hang in there and wait.

The "What-if?" Strategy

A popular strategy in sales negotiation that is used by both salespeople and buyers is the "What-if?" strategy. The salesperson says, "What if we substitute Grade A for Grade B at the same price?" The attractiveness of this strategy is that there's no commitment to enter such a contract but it still tests the reactions of the other party. If the prospect answers the salesperson in the example with, "Then we'll take it," the salesperson can consider it a sale and proceed to write it up, or can say, "Well, let me check to see if I can make the switch."

The prospect can use the "What-if?" strategy, too, as illustrated in Chapter 2. In fact, buyers tend to use it more than sellers. The prospect says, "What if we agree to give you a one-year contract?" The assumption is that the salesperson will shave the price a bit in return for the sale and the contract. The prospect still doesn't have to go through with the proposition, but one assumes that the party posing the "what if?" intends to go through with it if the response is acceptable.

Unfortunately, some buyers have a way of driving salespeople mad with a barrage of "what-if?" statements that nibble away at the price. The best way to protect yourself against rash responses to these "what-if?" tactics is to know your pricing schedule and all the limits. Don't give your answer too quickly. Do your calculations first and don't hesitate to check with higher authority.

You can take the "what-if?" idea a step further by answering with one of your own as an alternative. "Well, I'm not sure about that. But let me ask you this. What if we would recarpet the entrance foyer?"

"If I — will you?" "If you — then I"

There are any number of variations you can use that are comparable in purpose to the "What-if" strategy. One of the more common formats for salespeople goes this way. "If I can get our installers to agree to put the carpet down next Saturday while your office is closed, will you sign the order?" "If you can arrange for your truck to pick up the equipment at our warehouse, then I think I can reduce the cost by $132. Can you do that?"

Take a Break

When an important decision becomes necessary in a sales negotiation, the salesperson should consider taking a break before making it. The psychological pressure to get the negotiation over and the sale made is often too great to make a fully objective decision.

Taking a recess in the negotiation to think things over or to check with other people is an acceptable strategy.

Professional negotiators normally have a credible reason for taking a break in the negotiations. They are careful that the request doesn't indicate personal inability to make decisions. Salespeople use the break to discuss a proposal with higher authority if it contains conditions beyond the salesperson's authority to grant. "I think I understand your proposal, Mr. Stuart. Let me talk it over with my sales manager and explain it to him. May I get back to you at ten tomorrow?"

As mentioned previously, both salespeople and buyers find protection behind a lack of authority to grant excessive concessions.

Take the Edge Off of Hard Facts

Sometimes you have to give the buyer some solid facts during the course of the sales negotiation. If given in a too forceful manner, the buyer might be irritated.

Here are some examples that could turn the buyer off.

"You're smart enough to know that every day you operate this equipment as it is you're losing more than a hundred dollars."

"Well, I happen to know that you paid $12 for the ones you have now."

"I'm sure you wouldn't want your boss to know that you're endangering those records by saving a few bucks on the cabinets."

Using questions or qualifying statements tends to take the edge off of the same presentation of facts.

Let's see how that would work in the same examples. "How much do you figure you're losing each day without this collator on your equipment?"

"I'm guessing you paid about $12 for these, am I in the ball park?"

"After a fire destroyed your records, how do you think your boss would react to your telling him you saved $200 by not buying fire resistant files?"

It helps to suggest that your facts about the buyer's situation may not be entirely accurate, like, "Please correct me if I don't have this right." "Could I ask you a few questions to see if I have my facts correct?"

Don't Counterattack — Sidestep

In sales negotiations, the customer frequently takes a firm position and refuses to change. If you criticize the position or keep attacking it, the customer has to dig in to defend the position. Rather than push back or counterattack, the salesperson will get better response by sidestepping the position instead.

Don't reject or accept the customer's position or defend your own ideas when challenged. Use questions to get answers rather than just more resistance. "I can understand how you might feel that way, Miss Taylor. Let me ask you this. If I could come up with a way to fit this into your budget, would you be willing to consider it?" "Yes, the price is a little higher for this quality of paper. Let me ask, how do you intend to use the mailing piece?"

Ask questions that draw the prospect out. Then listen to the replies to identify a clue as to the prospect's possible reaction to another proposal or concession.

We will discuss suggestions for using questioning and listening more effectively during sales negotiations in Chapters 11 and 12.

Don't Let an Impasse Stop You

If you and the prospect or customer can't agree on one element of the sales proposal, that's no reason to consider the whole negotiation over.

Suggest that you go on to the other details and come back to the impasse later. "Let's shelve the topic of training your employees to use the equipment for the moment and go on to which model would best suit your operation."

Testing — Testing — Testing

In some kinds of selling where the price is highly adjustable, as in real estate, artwork or automobiles, both the buyer and the salesperson like to test the willingness of the other party to go for a given price.

The buyer wants to know how low the seller will go. The seller wants to know how much the buyer is willing to pay. When these limits are established, the possibility of further negotiations can be determined.

Strangely enough, a simple question often works as well as all the subterfuges. "Tell me honestly, now, what is the lowest price you will take?" asks the potential buyer. "What is your top budget figure for your kitchen renovation?" asks the salesman for kitchen cabinets.

Many buyers and sellers would like to get the whole negotiation over with and will give a reasonably honest reply that sets the level for further negotiations.

How to find the prospect's limit

Here are some tactics that work under some conditions for getting the buyer to express a limit.

1. *Use the "what-if?" tactic.* "What if we included the appliances, would you go to that amount?"

2. *After giving a price that is obviously high, ask what the buyer is willing to pay.* This will normally be too low, so the salesperson admits to being out of the running but engages the buyer in friendly conversation to establish the real limit. If that appears to be within the salesperson's range, he or she comes back with another bid.

3. *Use another sale as an example.* "We enclosed the Walton's porch for $4,700. Is that within your budget?"

4. *Start with the higher-priced article to test the prospect's intentions.* "No, that's more than I want to pay. Do you have a lower-priced one?"

5. *Watch for the buyer who will use the previous tactic in reverse.* The buyer shows interest in the lower quality item, then tries to get the better one at the same price.

HOW TO HANDLE QUESTIONS
DURING THE SALES NEGOTIATION

Asking questions is a great tool for salespeople, so much so that the entire Chapter 11 is devoted to the techniques for using them during negotiations. But they are an equally effective tool for the buyer to use during negotiations.

You can assume that the professional buyer will have had experience and even training in the use of questions to evaluate the proposals of salespeople and to gain concessions. How you answer these questions can very well determine the outcome of the sales negotiation.

There is a great temptation to give a quick answer to the prospect's question. It shows that we are masters of the subject.

Unfortunately, few of us are masters at quick thinking. A better answer often comes to us after the session starting with the thought, "I should have said . . ." Good preparation is the obvious solution to answering questions properly. A certain amount of preparation is possible by anticipating questions that might be asked or by writing down the stickler questions that were asked by previous buyers.

The more time you have to think about it, the better the answer should be.

Skill in answering questions involves knowing what not to say as well as what to say. Avoiding an answer is also an answer as any follower of negotiations and inquiries has discovered.

14 Suggestions for Handling Questions

Here are some suggestions for answering or fielding the questions buyers ask.

1. *Make sure you understand the question.* Ask the buyer to repeat it if you're not sure. "Would you mind repeating the question?" "I don't quite understand your question, Mr. Nolan."

2. *Take time to think through your answer.* "Let me think about that a moment. I want to be sure to give you the right information." "Let me check a chart here before I give you that figure."

3. *Qualify your answer if necessary.* "Before I answer that, let me point out that . . ." "Let me tell you the history on that before I give you a specific answer."

4. *You can legitimately refuse to answer some questions.* "I'm sure you don't expect me to give you that information, Mr. Walker (with a smile)." "I can't answer that because . . ."

5. *Postpone your answer if you don't have all the facts.* "That's a good question, but I don't have the answer at this moment. But let me call the office and try to get it for you if you like."

6. *Don't elaborate on answers to meaningless questions.* "Yes, that's true. Now let's consider another aspect of your problem."

7. *If the buyer interrupts your answer, let him or her talk.* It may affect your answer or nullify it entirely.

8. *You can answer part of a question without covering all of it.* "We can definitely deliver it to your Cleveland warehouse, but I'm not sure about using United Trucking."

9. *If the question is too general, give a specific answer.* "Well, let me give you a specific example of how we handled that for another customer."

10. *If the question is too specific, give a more general answer.* "Well, as a general rule, the results will work this way."

11. *If the question is loaded, unload it before answering it.* "Without placing the blame on anyone for a moment, let me say that . . ."

12. *Before answering a multiple question, break it down into its parts.* "To answer your first question, yes, we do allow an assortment of sizes. As to packaging, we . . ."

13. *If you feel you must evade a question, try answering an unasked question instead.* "That's a matter of opinion. Here's what we did for a customer who had the problem of intermittant leakage."

14. *Turn statements into questions so they avoid arguments.* "You make a good point. Do you need the larger model? That's the question, isn't it?" This is a tactic used in handling objections as discussed further in Chapter 9.

Don't Divulge Your Cost Breakdown

A favorite tactic of buyers who ask for proposals is to ask the salesperson for a breakdown of costs for the activities in the proposal. If the salesperson is naive enough to provide it, the buyer can see what the costs would be, where the profit is built in and how much it is. This tells him how far he can go in getting a better price by getting other bids on the materials and taking away some of the profit.

When the buyer asks for your cost breakdown, this is one question to politely refuse to answer. "I'm sorry, Mr. Adams. I'm not permitted to give that information, but you can be sure that we have kept all the costs in line with the quality you should have so that we could give you a fair price."

When You Close the Negotiation, Quit Talking and Get Out!

One of the important rules successful salespeople have learned is to quit talking and leave as soon as the sale is completed. The same advice is given by the experts in negotiation of any form.

Too many salespeople have talked themselves out of a sale by saying things needlessly that caused the buyer to change his or her mind and refuse to buy. "We're starting our fall sale next month so I'll get in touch with you then." "Is that so? Well, I'll wait until then to place my order because I don't need most of the things right now."

Just remaining in the presence of the buyer a little too long after getting the order gives the buyer an opportunity to have second thoughts. "Oh, I'm glad you're still here. I just remembered something the manager said a few weeks ago. I'd better not go ahead with the order until I check with him again. I'll call you next week. Thanks for coming in."

When you get the order, thank the buyer and get out!

PUTTING YOUR SELLING AND
NEGOTIATING SKILLS TOGETHER

In Part II, we cover ways to integrate the selling skills and techniques used by successful salespeople with the sales negotiation skills we have covered in Part I. To help you make this important integration, we review the reasons in Chapter 5 why people buy anything, why they are willing to negotiate with salespeople for the products and services that will satisfy their wants, needs and desires.

In Chapter 6 we cover the preparation and planning stage for the sales negotiation. Chapters 7 through 10 discuss the combining of selling and negotiating strategies starting with opening the sale, then making the sales presention, handling resistance and finally closing the sales negotiation.

Start with a good prospect

Finding and qualifying good prospects is highly important in most selling programs, but negotiation skills are rarely used in this activity except occasionally to set up a key appointment. For this reason, The Prospecting stage will not be covered. We will assume that you have found and qualified a good prospect and are now ready to prepare for the sales negotiation with that prospect.

Ask questions

Professional salespeople use questions skillfully to uncover and identify the prospect's needs, problems and desires and to get opinions that will guide the salesperson in making recommendations that will result in a sale. They use questions to get and hold the prospect's attention and to guide decision-making.

Many examples of the use of questions in each step of the sale are provided throughout Part II to show how they help integrate your negotiation techniques with your selling skills.

Then listen!

Effective listening skills are also highly important for salespeople. Asking questions and then not listening properly to the customer's reply obviously reduces the major benefit of asking the question.

Listening skills are also important in detecting clues a prospect or customer sends out that the salesperson can use to adjust the sales presentation and to identify specific benefits the prospect would especially desire. Listening skills are so important in selling that many companies provide special training in effective listening for their salespeople through workshops and a variety of courses.

Asking the right kind of questions and the ability to listen for important clues are so important in sales negotiation that we have devoted two complete chapters to these skills as Part III and Chapters 11 and 12.

Combining Your Selling and Negotiating Techniques

Let's go on to Part II and see how you can combine the sales negotiation techniques you have learned with the best selling techniques today's professional salespeople are using.

As you go through each Chapter, try to visualize yourself in that stage of your coming sales call. . . planning, opening, making a presentation, handling resistance and closing. Evaluate the suggestions given in the Chapter in terms of your own typical selling situation. When a suggestion seems worthwhile, make a commitment to yourself to try it out at the next appropriate sales call.

Your HANDBOOK for Sales Negotiation

While planning an important call, refer to this book to refresh your memory on how you can improve your sales negotiation position and strategy.

As you increase your sales negotiation power and skills, you will find yourself closing more and more sales. That is what makes the extra effort pay off!

BIBLIOGRAPHY

The following books on general negotiation are recommended by the author for salespeople who want to broaden their background on the subject. They will have suggestions which can be utilized by salespeople as well as buyers because they are aimed to help any person who is involved in any form of government, labor, business or personal negotiation.

Much of the emphasis in books and courses on general negotiation is on helping the consumer negotiate better terms in purchasing and in the many difficult and frustrating situations one faces in life. Salespeople will benefit, of course, because they are also consumers and face personal problems where general negotiating know-how can help. But more important, they will be better prepared in a selling situation to cope with the tactics the buyers who have training in negotiation will use. (A digest of typical buyer strategies and tactics in sales negotiation and how to cope with them is provided in Chapter 2.)

Seminars, workshops and package courses in negotiation are offered to companies and individuals. Authors Herb Cohen, Chester and Gary Karrass, and Gerard Nierenberg listed below are popular in this field. Many firms provide this training to salespeople as well as the purchasing executives.

Recommended References on Negotiation

Brooks, Earl and Odiorne, George. *Managing by Negotiations.* Van Nostrand Reinhold. 1984.

Cohen, Herb. *You Can Negotiate Anything.* Bantam. 1982.

Fisher, Roger and Ury, William. *Getting To Yes.* Penguin. 1983.

Hanan, Mack, Cribbin, James and Berrian, Howard. *Sales Negotiation Strategies.* Amacom. 1977.

Ilich, John. *The Art and Skill of Successful Negotiation.* Bengal Press. 1983.

Karrass, Chester. *The Negotiating Game.* Thomas Crowell. 1970.

Karrass, Chester. *Give and Take.* Thomas Crowell. 1974.

Karrass, Gary. *Negotiate to Close.* Simon and Schuster. 1985.

Lewis, David. *Power Negotiating Tactics and Techniques.* Prentice-Hall. 1984.

Nierenberg, Gerard I. *The Art of Negotiating.* Cornerstone. 1981.

Schatzki, Michael and Coffey, Wayne. *Negotiation, the Art of Getting What You Want.* Signet. 1981.

PART II:

Combining Your Negotiating and Selling Skills to Close More Sales

5
Why Buyers Negotiate

No Buying Motive, No Negotiation

NO SALE was ever negotiated without a buying motive. Human needs and the satisfaction of those needs are the basis for any kind of negotiation. In sales negotiation, human physical and emotional needs become buying motives.

Sales negotiation becomes a matter of the parties saying, "If you help me satisfy my needs to this extent, I'll help you satisfy yours to this extent." The language actually comes out something like this, "If you'll install the door in addition to these other items at the same price, you've got a deal."

There's no point in entering the sales negotiation unless both parties want to satisfy a need, so it's important that each tries to indentify the primary needs of the other party.

One might assume that the needs of salespeople in the sales negotiation are reasonably clear, to increase their income by making a sale. Yet professional buyers who have taken courses in negotiation know that they can appeal to personal needs other than making money when trying to get favorable concessions.

Depending on the circumstances, these could include needs like job security, saving of time, pride in making a big sale, prestige or social approval.

Salespeople have a more difficult time, however, in determining the specific needs and buying motives of the buyers, so we will discuss some of the ways for identifying them and appealing to them.

Nothing Is Ever Bought Without a Buying Motive

Nothing is ever bought without a buying motive, yet the buyer is seldom aware of why he or she really bought. I own a native African drum made out of a genuine hyena skin. Every time I look at it I wonder why I ever bought it, and I'm sure that visitors who say, "Isn't that interesting," wonder the same thing.

But the experts in motivation will say that at the moment I negotiated with the flea market merchant for that drum, it satisfied a basic emotional need or buying motive. While I can't identify it now, the salesman undoubtedly did and that was all that mattered to make the sale.

WHAT DO PEOPLE BUY?

Although sales negotiations involve agreements on features of the product or service, particularly price, service and delivery, professional salespeople understand one important rule about buying motives:

A person's reason for buying is NEVER the mere desire to own the product itself but rather what the product will DO to satisfy a basic need.

People don't buy paint, they buy beauty and protection of property. They don't buy life jackets, they buy safety and comfort. They don't buy gloves, they buy protection, comfort or social approval.

Successful salespeople emphasize the BENEFITS their product delivers which answer the buyer's needs rather than the product itself.

What is your product worth in the sales negotiation? Only what the buyer feels about it. How much the buyer is willing to give up in money and effort, is equal to the total amount of BENEFITS the buyer and the firm or family expects to receive from the product or service.

Appeal to the Buying Motives?

Motivation research, finding out why people buy, has contributed greatly to modern marketing of products and services. Many texts have been written on buyer motivation and types of buyer personalities. Good sales training courses use the findings of this research in preparing salespeople to understand why people buy so they can develop their presentations to appeal to the customer's buying motives.

You Don't Have to be a Psychiatrist

You don't have to have a degree in psychiatry to be a salesperson, but you can utilize the facts the experts have found to be true about all of us when it comes to physical and emotional needs and wants . . . our buying motives.

There are many books available on the psychological aspects of selling. Most of them offer theories and formulas for placing labels on both buyers and salespeople as to their emotional needs and probable reactions to a given approach.

Through the use of charts and grids, the salesperson is supposed to be able to predict how the buyer will react to different approaches during the sales negotiation. Other systems offer to help the salespeople analyze their own personalities to see how a given personality will affect the response of each of the various customers types.

Some firms give their sales force intensive training in the use of the grids and customer analysis. Given enough time for study, experimentation and experience, I'm sure that salespeople would be able to do a better analysis of the buyers they face in sales negotiation.

No Time for Games During the Sales Negotiation

I have enjoyed using the charts and grids that are designed to help salespeople identify the various types of customers they will meet and to predict how each might react to a given presentation and to the salesperson's own personality projection. It makes an interesting game.

I have found, however, that typical salespeople do not have the time or opportunity to analyze the buyers they meet or give them a tag and plot them on a grid before entering the sales situation.

More important, I've found that even those salespeople who have learned to identify and classify customer types aren't sure what special handling to give them during the sales negotiation.

A Better Solution: Play the Averages

My solution, and the one found usuable for the majority of professional salespeople, is to play the averages as far as buying motives go.

In sales negotiation, you are more interested in knowing WHAT buyers are most apt to do rather than WHY they do it.

Most people have similar buying motives although they will differ in what they feel will best satisfy those needs. The typical buyer's behavior seems to be fairly predictable even though that of a single individual might be different.

In preparing for the sales presentation, salespeople identify those basic buying motives best served by their product or service. During the presentation, and later in the negotiation stage, professional sales negotiators emphasize the benefits their product will produce that match the basic buying motives, like pleasure, profit or prestige. Through probing questions and listening, they are able to better identify the specific buying motives most important to the individual buyer, like saving time in handling the accounts receivable.

THE 6 BASIC BUYING MOTIVES

Shown here is a chart of basic buying motives that I developed over the years from reading a wide variety of studies by experts and from picking the brains of psychologists and respected sales trainers for ideas that seemed to make sense.

In addition to the primary desire of survival, I have determined that there are just six basic buying motives that are popularly accepted. Four are often mentioned in pairs because they are related positively and negatively: Fear of Loss and Hope of Gain; Pleasure and the Avoidance of Pain. The other two are Pride and Desire for Approval.

I'm sure that these basic buying motives could have more scientific-sounding names, and I know that more have been identified in the various texts on selling and human behavior. But all of the buying motives mentioned can usually be placed within the framework of these six basic buying motives.

In the chart, examples of specific buying motives are shown following each basic buying motive. Some are related to two or more. Good health, for example, can contribute to all six basic motives although it is probably most positively linked to Pleasure. That's why the advertisers prefer to say, "It's fun to be healthy," instead of "Save money on doctor bills." You can expand the list of examples by identifying more specific needs and desires that will better fit your own product or service, like "more miles per gallon." But until you know more about your specific buyer, these basic buying motives will help you play the averages most successfully.

4 Ways to Determine a Prospect's Buying Motives

When salespeople discover what the prospect really wants, the primary buying motive, they have the key to making the sale.

They have to determine which of the buying motives will have the greatest effect on the prospect's decision to buy and which one is the strongest at the moment. Knowing that, they will emphasize the features of their product or service and their benefits that will best satisfy the prospect's predominate buying motives.

But how can you locate your prospect's strongest buying motives? Here are four ways.

1. Ask questions. "If I could help you save three minutes on each machine operation, would you be interested?"

2. Listen for volunteered comments. For example, if the prospect says, "I wish I had more time to go camping," the salesperson might emphasize the labor-saving, time-saving benefits that result from using the product.

THE 6 BASIC BUYING MOTIVES

Basic Buying Motive	Examples of Specific Buying Motive
1. Profit or Gain	Save money; make money; economy; more profit; more sales; longer wear; personal advancement.
2. Fear of Loss	Reduce costs; prevent loss; guarantee; safety; save time; protect property, health or loved ones; long wear; security; no risk; no blame; insurance.
3. Comfort and Pleasure	Enjoyment; good health; comfort; good food and drink; good housing; beauty; sexual attraction; entertainment; sports; recreation; improved employee morale; keep and attract better employees.
4. Avoidance of Pain	Protection; relief from pain; less work; save time; security; safety; good health; no worry; more attractive; reduce loss.
5. Love and Affection	Family; social approval; beauty; admiration; security of loved ones; loyalty; friendship; better public relations; better employee relations.
6. Pride and Prestige	Social acceptance; desire to possess; style; fashion; high quality; learning; advancement; admiration; imitation; self- improvement; honors; recognition; leadership; improved product; beat competition; higher sales; good public image.

3. Listen to comments during the presentation. The auto customer asks, "How fast will it go?" Now the salesperson can assume that the prospect is more interested in speed or prestige than in economy of operation.

4. Observe. Study the prospects, their surroundings, evidence of hobbies, products they now use.

SELL THE BENEFITS

Sales training in recent years has stressed the Feature/Benefit strategy in making sales presentations and in the handling of resistance and closings. In the interest of space, we'll just review the principles as they apply to sales negotiation.

The Feature/Benefit system of selling is based on the fact that people do not buy things or products, they buy what the product will DO for them in solving one or more of their buying motives, their needs and desires.

The salesperson points out the features of the product, like "makes copies faster," but immediately converts the feature into a user benefit, like "so you'll save waiting time and labor costs."

The salesperson has to come into the sales negotiation not only with a good knowledge of the features of the product but also with a predetermination of the benefits he or she will emphasize during the presentation and negotiation for that particular buyer.

Preparation for the Feature/Benefit presentation can be a simple worksheet divided into two columns, one headed Features and the other, Benefits. The salesperson simply lists the product features or characteristics in the first column, then after each one the benefits the buyer will receive because of that feature.

The benefits will be like those shown on the Basic Buying Motives chart, for example, saves money, increases profit, tastes better, lasts longer, reduces accidents.

So what?

While practicing converting product features into user benefits in our workshops, we found it helpful to imagine the customers with a sign on their foreheads saying, "So what?". The salespeople were asked to keep answering the question until the basic buying motive was reached.

For example, "The chair has aluminum legs." "So what?" "So they won't rust." "So what?" So you won't have to replace the chairs as often." "So what?" "So you'll save money." "Oh!"

Inevitably a salesperson would remark that any prospect that doesn't realize he would save money if a product costs less per ounce than a competitive product would have to be pretty stupid. And of course, that would be true IF the prospect were listening intently. But you can't be sure. The added statement, "So you'll save money," takes only seconds more and makes sure the buyer identifies the product with a reason for buying. Why take a chance?

8 Guidelines for Negotiating the Benefits

Here are some ideas and observations associated with benefit selling that should be considered while making the sales presentation and during the negotiations that follow.

1. *People do not buy until they realize that a product fulfills a specific buying motive.* The reason for buying will never be the desire to own the product itself. It will be to gain some benefit which the product provides and which matches the buying motive. Think of the buyer saying, "Don't tell me how good your products are. Tell me how good they will make me feel."

2. *The customer is not interested in the features of a product but rather in the benefits which these features will produce.* Make sure your prospects associate the product with the benefits it will produce when they own it.

People don't buy a specific television set because it has a unique picture tube. They buy the pleasure of watching the better picture which the tube produces.

3. *Everything we do is related to our own personal interests.* Even our actions in behalf of others, our sacrifices of time, energy and love, give us personal satisfaction as a means of compensation.

For salespeople this means that prospects will buy only if it is in their self-interest. Even buyers for a business firm are influenced by how they will benefit personally in increased prestige, job security, chances for advancement, or just the personal satisfaction of negotiating a successful contract.

So it might help if you can conveniently mention, "I'm sure your supervisor will be delighted to know you were able to get higher quality ductwork at the same price."

4. *More sales are based on emotional response than on logic.* More cars are bought for their styling, for prestige and pleasure than as an answer to a transportation problem. Appeal to logic if you can, but use emotional appeals to clinch the benefits.

5. *A person's preference for satisfying needs is influenced by priorities of the moment.* A man who wasn't interested in a diamond ring yesterday can be found looking into a jewelry store window today because of events that

changed his perspective last night. An industrial buyer who wasn't interested in your product during the last call may have different buying motive priorities today because of a meeting of the sales and marketing staff yesterday.

6. *A person can be convinced that a product will satisfy a need quite well and still not buy.* Often several buying motives compete within the buyer's mind and the strongest ones at the moment win out. A fudge sundae will certainly satisfy the desire for pleasure, and the price may be right.

But the other long range desires for such things as sexual attraction, social acceptance or good health that come with fewer calories may overrule the prospect's immediate desire for pleasure. At some other time, the fudge sundae may win out. A person might have a strong desire to save money, yet a salesperson might have trouble selling him an elephant even at a tremendous savings.

There must be a favorable balance of reasons for buying and for not buying.

7. *A person can be convinced that a product will satisfy a need and not be willing to take the pain of parting with the money it will cost.* He or she may prefer to spend the same amount of money to satisfy other needs that are more powerful at the moment.

8. *The behavior of people on the average is fairly predictable even though that of a single individual might not be.* Many factors shape each person's desires and values and thus their buying motives. These include heredity, environment, education, experience, social status and income.

Since few people have these in the same proportion and exact quality, everyone has a different idea on what product best satisfies their particular buying motive. Some will think it's your product and some won't. Play the averages until you determine that you are dealing with a unique buyer.

Use Features for Proof

While we emphasize the need for selling the benefit the product produces rather than the product itself, we don't want to imply that salespeople should leave out any mention of the product features that create the benefits. On the contrary, features form an important part of the sales presentation and the negotiation that follows.

They become the PROOF for the buyer that the benefit will be forthcoming after the purchase.

It is probably not a big secret that buyers don't always believe the statements made by salespeople. So just in case your prospect or customer might feel that your promise of certain benefits is a bit exaggerated, link the feature to the benefit as proof.

A key word used by the professional salesperson to establish the proof is "because." For example, the salesperson says, "This tire reduces the danger of skids BECAUSE the tread cannot squeeze shut," or, "You will save on shipping costs BECAUSE our new plastic container is ten times lighter than a glass bottle."

While it seems more effective to give the benefit of ownership first, the salesperson can also give the feature first. In this case, the word "so" becomes the key linking word. Using the previous example, it might go like this. "Our new plastic container is ten times lighter than a glass bottle, SO you will save on your shipping costs."

Remember these key words, BECAUSE and SO. They will remind you to always link the customer benefit with the feature which provides the proof.

Ask If the Buyer Wants the BENEFIT, Not the FEATURE

Some time ago while conducting a series of workshops called "Persuasive Selling," we discussed and role played the use of questions to persuade the prospect to make decisions which would lead to the final sale.

One day, while studying the more effective questions that came out of the groups, an important strategy became apparent to me. When used in the workshops that followed, the strategy proved itself a valuable guideline for persuasive questioning by the salespeople. It is:

"Always ask the prospects if they want the BENEFITS, rather than if they want the FEATURES of the product."

Going back to the tire salesperson in the example, he might have asked a question like, "Now this tire has the new XY tread design. Would you prefer it?"

Compare that with this question. "How do you feel about tires that reduce the danger of skids?" The container salesperson might have asked, "Wouldn't you prefer a lighter container?" Compare that with, "Are you interested in finding ways to reduce shipping costs?"

It's easy to say you don't want or aren't concerned with the features of a product like stainless steel, a reinforcement, lighter weight or whatever. But who can say they aren't interested in the benefits like saving time, saving money, making more profit, having more pleasure, less pain?

When you get down to the negotiation level and are closing the sale, you obviously have to ask if the buyer prefers one feature over another, like chrome plating or enamel.

But by this time, you should have helped the buyer make the right decisions through questions that asked about wanting the benefits rather than
the product features themselves.

Fight Price Resistance With Benefits

Price is the major subject for sales negotiation. But it's important to
remember that nobody buys anything because of its price. They buy it only
because of the benefits they will enjoy through owning the product or using
the service. The price the buyers will pay is also matched in their minds by
the sum total of the strengths of the benefits they will receive for that price.
That's why successful sales negotiators review the features and benefits
when quoting a price. "The price is just $750 and that includes this faster
feed that will save you time and labor costs."

Conversely, when making price concessions that take away features and
benefits, emphasize what the buyer will be giving up just to get a lower
price. "Yes, we can reduce the price of the package by $264 if you are
willing to give up the sheet feeder that allows you to use cut paper on your
printer."

More About Benefit Negotiation Later

The principles involved in why people buy, and in benefit selling, apply
to the whole selling process. So we will refer to them again as we discuss
each of the stages of the sale in the remaining sections.

You may want to refer to this section for review as we discuss new applications of the principles and give additional ideas and suggestions for their
use in persuading buyers during the sales negotiation.

6
Planning the Sales Negotiation

Be Ready to Negotiate

SALES negotiation requires advance planning just as any other form of negotiation. You can be sure that General Motors and the United Auto Workers don't wait until the last day before the contract expires to start their planning for the labor contract negotiations.

For salespeople, just as for General Motors, planning for sales negotiation is a year-round function.

The success of professional salespeople depends largely upon their skill in planning as well as in conducting each sales call. They leave nothing to chance that they can cover before they meet the buyer face-to-face.

Like any other successful businessman, the salesperson sets an objective for each call and develops the strategy that will be used to obtain this objective.

The effectiveness of the strategy you develop for each sales call depends upon your ability to predict the situation at the time of the call and to take control of the negotiation.

If you have regular customers, you are continually collecting information about their needs, problems, applications, changes in personnel, markets, anything that will affect your ongoing sales negotiations with them.

Develop the Game Plan

Once the strategy is determined, professional salespeople select the tactics that they believe will result in winning the objective. These are the specific things they will say, what they will do, and how they will do it when face-to-face with the buyer.

While the effectiveness of the sales negotiation depends considerably on how well it has been planned, it seldom goes exactly as planned. That's why salespeople have to pay close attention to the buyer during the negotiation and use what they see and hear to adjust their tactics accordingly.

In order to make adjustments in their planned presentation, they must understand the buyers and how to influence them. The final test of the salesperson's ability is the extent to which he or she can control the sales negotiation without seeming to do so.

We have discussed the many reasons why people buy, and will discuss techniques for persuading them to do so in the sections which follow.

Using these suggestions will help you develop a personal reservoir of tactics that permit you to persuade the buyer to move in the direction of the final sale no matter how your initial plan makes out during the sales negotiation.

Areas for Planning Your Sales Negotiation Strategy

In planning your overall sales negotiation strategy, you must consider the stages through which your sale will progress. Each of these stages requires a different strategy to reach the objective, but all of them must lead toward the final objective, the completed sale.

There are hundreds of good textbooks on selling and a wide variety of courses that are available for salespeople. Individual companies have in-house initial training courses as well as continuous, upgrading courses for their salespeople. It is not our purpose here to challenge any selling method or to present a new one. We simply want to review the generally accepted basics of good selling and show how modern negotiation techniques can be added to increase the odds of sales success.

As we discuss the basic stages through which the typical sale progresses, we ask that you relate your own special selling techniques to them. Keep in mind that our objective is to add the strategies and tactics of negotiation wherever appropriate.

THE 6 BASIC STAGES IN THE TYPICAL SALE

Individual authors of textbooks may identify the stages in selling by different names and may break them down into sub-stages. But most experts seem to agree that any salesperson planning the total sales strategy must consider a minimum of six basic stages through which the sale must progress on the way to completion.

If you have a favorite formula, compare it with these stages.

Stage 1. Prospecting. Salespeople must continually find and qualify prospects. No prospect, no sales negotiation.

Stage 2. Planning the call. The salesperson collects information about the buyer, the problems, needs and desires that can be resolved by the salesperson's product or service. Some texts call this planning and collection stage the Pre-approach because it takes place before the actual Approach to the buyer.

From the information obtained, the negotiation power balance can be estimated and the strategy for the negotiation planned.

Stage 3. The approach. The salesperson gets the interview with the buyer and finally meets him or her face-to-face. The tactics for getting the buyer's quick and favorable attention and stimulating his or her interest in finding out more about the proposition is very important.

If it fails, the rest of the planning for the sales interview cannot be effective and there will be no opportunity for negotiation.

Stage 4. The presentation. The salesperson acquaints the buyer with the product or service, demonstrates the features and shows how they will produce benefits for the buyer or the firm. During the presentation the salesperson asks questions and listens to the buyer's remarks that help qualify the buyer, uncover special interests, needs, problems and preferences that will aid in the negotiation phase.

At the end of the presentation, the salesperson makes a proposal and moves into the Closing stage.

Stage 5. Negotiating resistance. Salespeople anticipate resistance to their closing attempt and plan their strategy for handling it. Through probing tactics, they uncover objections so they can be negotiated satisfactorily.

Stage 6. Closing the sale. After the presentation and after handling any objection or resistance, the salesperson uses planned strategies for helping the buyer make decisions that will ultimately result in the sale.

The strategies salespeople can use in the final five of these six stages in a typical sales negotiation will be discussed in more detail in the Chapters which follow. We will assume that you have done your Prospecting, the important first stage but one that involves little negotiation.

We will start with your Approach stage in Chapter 7 in which you make your first call on those qualified prospects and lay the groundwork for the coming negotiations.

Meanwhile, let's consider what the experts say goes on in the mind of the buyer during the stages of the sales interview that affects the outcome of the sale. Refer to the chart which follows to get a better understanding of how all the elements of the sale fit together.

The 5 Mental Steps to a Sale

Sales psychologists give different labels to the mental steps a customer takes before buying anything. We can simplify all these opinions by saying that the salesperson needs to grasp the prospect's mind and lead it through five basic mental steps before any sale can be made.

The names given to these steps are common to most sales training texts and programs, but there is sometimes confusion among salespeople on how they relate to the basic stages the salesperson goes through during the sale.

The chart which follows was developed for our seminars to help show the relationships between the stages of the sale and the mental steps the prospect must take during them. Refer to it as you identify these basic mental steps.

Step 1. Attention. The salesperson must get and hold the buyer's favorable attention.

Step 2. Interest. The salesperson must arouse the prospect's interest in learning more about the proposition.

Step 3. Conviction. The salesperson must convince the buyer that he or she has a need that could be satisfied by the salesperson's product or service.

Step 4. Desire. The salesperson must persuade the buyer to satisfy the need with the product or service.

Step 5. Action. The salesperson helps the customer decide to take definite action that results in a sale.

Let's Go to the Sales Negotiation Formula Chart

Let's see how the prospect's five mental steps relate to the six basic stages through which we have said the sales interview progresses. Refer to the Sales Negotiation Formula Chart and follow along.

The first physical contact with the buyer is made during the third stage of the sale, the Approach.

In a matter of seconds, the salesperson must get the buyer's favorable Attention. Attention-getters are only temporary, however, so the salesperson must immediately strive to arouse the prospect's Interest in hearing more about the proposition.

In a good sales interview, it is difficult to tell when Attention gives way to Interest. While that's not important, it is important that you hold the buyer's attention all through the sales interview.

The strength of the buyer's Interest depends upon how well you appeal to his or her buying motives discussed in Chapter 5. During the Planning

THE SALES NEGOTIATION FORMULA

Stages in the Sale	Prospect's Mental Steps		Prospect Decisions
1. PROSPECTING Salesperson locates and qualifies prospect. Gets interviews.			
2. PLANNING THE SALES NEGOTIATION Salesperson studies prospect's possible needs, problems, desires. Plans all stages in the sale. Assesses negotiation power balance.			
3. THE APPROACH Salesperson meets prospect in person. Gets favorable attention and stimulates interest in learning more about the salesperson's proposition.	Attention Interest		Will I SEE this person? Will I LISTEN to him/her?
4. THE PRESENTATION Salesperson uncovers prospect's needs. Stimulates desire to have needs satisfied through demonstration of product/service. Makes trial close on proposal.	Interest Conviction Desire		Will I LISTEN to him/her? Do I NEED the benefits offered? Will the PRODUCT/SERVICE offered give me these benefits? Is this person the BEST SOURCE for the product/service? Is the PRICE reasonable?
5. NEGOTIATING RESISTANCE Salesperson probes for and listens to objections. Answers them, negotiates solutions and resells the benefits.		Conviction Desire	
6. CLOSING THE SALES NEGOTIATION Salesperson helps prospect make decision to buy now or to accept a proposal that could lead to a sale later.	Action		SHOULD I buy? Should I buy NOW?

stage, you determined how the prospect could benefit from buying your product or service. During the Opening of the sale and as the sales interview progresses, use probing questions to verify these and more specific buying motives. Ways to do this are covered in Chapter 7 and those which follow.

The mental process, Conviction, requires proof to the buyer that he or she has a need and that it can be satisfied with your product or service.

Demonstration, try-outs, testimonials, surveys, and questioning may be involved to prove the need exists and that you have a logical solution.

Unfortunately, even proof that the buyer needs what your product or service can provide is not enough to make the sale. We all have some needs we know about but are not motivated enough to satisfy. We're not willing to part with the money, time or trouble it would take to satisfy them, or we have other needs with greater priority.

The salesperson must create the Desire within the buyer to satisfy the need once the buyer is convinced he or she has it.

Desire has to be brought out through tactics similar to those used to get Conviction, like the demonstration, testimonials, surveys and questioning.

Hopefully, the Conviction and Desire will occur together. Desire is linked to the benefits resulting from owning the product rather than from the product itself. So you must take the buyers mentally into the future where they can visualize themselves or their firms enjoying those benefits.

We will discuss ways to develop and conduct the sales presentation so that it deals effectively with the buyer's mental decisions in Chapter 8.

Buyer Resistance Calls for Negotiation

Sometimes the buyer's Conviction and Desire occur quickly and the salesperson can close the sale on details like payment or delivery. This is what happens in retail stores with self-selection merchandising. The customer looks at the product, may read the label, is convinced the product will satisfy a need he wants satisfied, picks the item up and walks to the checkout counter to pay for it. For most sales where professional salespeople are involved, however, there comes a stage where the buyer resists buying for some reason and further selling and negotiation are required.

Professional salespeople anticipate buyer resistance and plan ahead with strategies for handling it. The strategy includes bringing the objections to buying out in the open so the salesperson can answer them and negotiate a solution.

As long as the buyer keeps the objections bottled up, the salesperson has no guidance for further persuasion or correction of misunderstanding. We will discuss specific strategies for handling and negotiating buyer resistance in Chapter 9.

Action Required to Close the Sale

The mental Action step is obviously part of the Closing stage of the sales negotiation. If all of the preceding four mental steps are handled properly, the Action step becomes a routine of agreeing on details and signing the order.

Unfortunately, the Closing stage often takes more of the kind of persuasion that was used in the Presentation and Negotiation stages. We will discuss the strategies for getting closing action more fully in Chapter 10.

The Buyer Has to Make 8 Important Decisions

While the salesperson is taking the buyer through the five mental steps to the sale, the buyer is mentally asking eight important questions whose answers will determine the progress as well as the final outcome of the sale. Whatever the strategies used during the sales interview and negotiation, you will not close the sale or get approval of your proposal unless you help the buyer say yes to all eight of these important questions.

Refer to the chart which shows the stages in the sales negotiation where these buyer decisions must be made.

1. Will I SEE this person?
2. Will I LISTEN to him/her?
3. Do I NEED the benefits offered?
4. Will the PRODUCT/SERVICE offered give me these benefits?
5. Is this person the BEST SOURCE for the product/service?
6. Is the PRICE reasonable?
7. SHOULD I buy?
8. Should I buy NOW?

Although the eight decisions will be made in approximately the order given here, some may already have been made before you arrive. Your first job is to determine which decisions have been made and what the answers are.

If you get the interview, you can assume the buyer has made the first decision in your favor. It doesn't mean that any of the others are in your favor, however.

Keep these buyer's questions in mind when planning your presentation and make sure you cover the factors during the presentation and negotiation that will influence yes answers to all the questions.

Putting It All Together

The Chapters which follow will discuss in more detail the stages of the typical sale and strategies for handling them. The Sales Negotiation Formula Chart shows how the buyer's reactions and decisions coincide with the six basic stages in the typical sales negotiation. These relationships should help you clarify the planning of your strategy and tactics in each stage down to the final sale.

THE PROBLEM-SOLVING APPROACH TO SALES NEGOTIATION

The professional sales negotiator is basically a problem-solver, not an order-taker. While this may be more apparent in the industrial and commercial selling fields, it is equally true at the higher levels of personal services like insurance or investing and the home markets like home-building and major appliances.

The problem-solving strategy is usually developed in the Planning stage following the decision to use it, but it is put into effect during the Prospecting stage where prospect problems are identified or suspected.

For example, hints of possible problems can come from research during the Prospecting stage through such things as news items about the prospect, common problems in the prospect's industry, mentions by present customers, and the salesperson's own experience solving customer problems. Having solved one customer's problem, for example, the professional salesperson looks around for prospects in the same business or neighborhood who could be having similar problems.

During the Opening of the sale, the salesperson uses questions that help to identify or verify the prospect's problem, then gets the prospect's agreement that the problem exists.

During the Presentation stage, the salesperson asks questions to refine and pinpoint the problem, then makes a proposal for resolving the problem. Hopefully, this leads to Closing the sale, but if not, then the sales negotiation phase takes place.

We will discuss the overall strategy of problem-solving selling here, then discuss some of the tactics used in the problem-solving approach as they relate to the specific stages of the sale in the Chapters which follow.

No Problem, No Sale

No one buys anything except to solve a problem, a need. Where there is no problem, there will be no sale. Think of anything you bought recently. You bought it to solve a problem you had either mentally or physically.

In retrospect, the purchase-solution might seem strange to you, but at the time you bought the product or service, it was the best solution you could find for what you were willing to pay to solve your problem. Customers and salespeople are partners in solving the problems, the buyer's needs.

In the Planning stage, professional salespeople try to visualize problems which the prospect might have which could be solved with the salesperson's product or service.

The search for problems to solve is obviously influenced by the nature of the product or service. Salespeople for road machinery will have a different approach to finding problems than will the salespeople for infant clothing. But each will research the prospects as much as possible to locate the problems before confronting them in the sales interview.

When the salespeople demonstrate to the buyers that they understand their problems, the buyers are more interested in hearing about the suggested solutions.

Whether you sell paper clips or computers, you will have to find a prospect with a PROBLEM that can be solved with a paper clip or a computer or you will never make a sale.

No Problem? Find One!

Progress toward a sale gets a good start when the prospects know they have a need or problem and admit it to the salespeople. But more often in higher bracket selling, the salesperson has to uncover a problem and tell the prospect about it. How do you do this? By observing the prospect's situation and asking questions. What is going on now that could be improved with your product or service? From your past experience, what problems did similar customers have that you solved for them? See if the same problems exist in the prospect's situation, then offer to solve them, too. Ask questions of acquaintances, competitors of the prospect, employees, anyone who might give you a clue to the problems now being experienced.

Got a Solution? Find the Matching Problem!

Your product or service are solutions to problems or needs. Look around to find prospects with these problems. When you get a new product, study what benefits it provides that will solve a problem for your customer.

THE 6 STEPS IN PROBLEM-SOLVING SELLING

Here are the six basic steps professional salespeople take in finding and solving problems for their prospects and customers. Some of these can be done in the planning stages. Some will have to be done during the opening of the sales call by questioning the customer and observing the operation.

Sometimes a request to make a survey is the preliminary step. The final two steps are the basis for the sales negotiation, making the proposal and negotiating the final sales contract.

Step 1. Identify the problem. Ask questions: What, Why, When, Where, Who and How? The key question is Why? Why is it done this way? Why does this happen? Listen to the answers to the questions to isolate the problem.

Step 2. Determine if the problem is worth solving. Problem-solving is the approach professional salespeople take for larger returns. But that doesn't mean that salespeople should try to solve every problem for their customers. They must first ask the question, "Will immediate or potential sales make it worth my time to find a solution to this problem?" If the answer is no, forget it.

Step 3. Determine the benefits. Salespeople must determine the anticipated benefits of the solution to both the firm and to the individual who will approve the order. There is no point in spending a lot of time improving and simplifying an operation that shouldn't be done at all. Look for the basic benefit, the objective, and aim the solution at it, not just the immediate problem.

Step 4. Consider all possible solutions. When you can visualize several solutions to a problem, consider and evaluate each one. Here is where you call upon your own knowledge and experience as well as others in your firm. Weigh the advantages and disadvantages of each against the benefits desired in a solution. Arrange the solutions in order of preference.

Step 5. Recommend a solution. The problem-solver salesperson will tell the buyer something like, "Based on what you have told me, I would suggest that WE do this." Another way is to bring in a third party to help validate the solution, like, "The ABC company had a similar problem and based on what we did for them, I suggest that WE . . ."

Step 6. Negotiate the solution. One great advantage of problem-solving selling is that when the buyer accepts your solution to the problem, the sale is usually assumed and the remaining negotiation is on details like price and delivery. This can be the answer to a simple question like, "When can we get started," or it could involve considerable give and take negotiation.

Armed with these solutions, try to uncover specific matching problems that people or firms in your area have. This should be part of the qualifying step in every salesperson's prospecting activity.

Gather Pre-negotiation Aids

Anything you can learn about the prospective buyer before going into the sales negotiation will be an advantage as brought out in Chapter 3. Some of this information you will uncover during your prospecting and qualifying stage. Some you will have to collect after qualifying the prospect as worthy of a sales call.

The information can be obtained in a variety of ways including the usual prospecting and qualifying sources, past experience with the buyer, other salespeople, by talking with friends and other employees of the prospect firm, reading the newspapers and industry literature, and even your competitors.

Some of the information can only be obtained during the actual call on the prospect during the Approach and Presentation stages.

Your Pre-negotiation Checklist

Here is a sample checklist of some areas where information would be helpful before sales negotiations start. You can add other questions to this list for your own planning based on your experience and that of others in selling your product or service.

1. What are the prospect's needs and desires that could be answered by your product or service?

2. What competitors' products is the prospect using now?

3. What has been the prospect's experience with a competitive product?

4. How do competitive products compare with yours? Advantages? Disadvantages?

5. What are the prospect's feelings about the present supplier?

6. What are the prospect's feelings about you or your company? What is your local reputation? Has there been any trouble between your firm and the prospect in the past?

7. What does the prospect already know about your product or service?

8. Are there any clues as to how the prospect feels about using your product or service?

9. What benefits might appeal to the buyer as a person as well as being a representative of the company?

10. Who do you know in common with the prospect that might provide a testimonial?

11. Do you have any customers or mutual acquaintances who might arrange for an appointment?

12. Which of your customers or past sales would most impress the prospect?

What is Your Power Relationship with the Prospect?

We said earlier that it pays to make an estimate of the relative balance of power between yourself and the prospect or customer before going into the sales negotiation. What are the advantages over the present operation you can exploit? What are the advantages you can expect the prospect or customer to use?

You can make a start on this assessment during the prospecting and qualifying stage by such actions as identifying the prospect's special needs and problems, by finding out who the present suppliers are, by getting an estimate of the buying power and the potential volume of your product or service you might expect if the sale were successful, and by learning all you can about the background of the firm and the individual with whom you will negotiate.

Review the types of strength you and the prospect may have going into the negotiation in Chapter 3. Be ready to use your strengths of product knowledge, expertise and experience, competitive advantages and persuasive and negotiation skills. Be alert to the prospect's typical strengths of being able to refuse to buy, being satisfied with present conditions and supplier, and possible negotiation skills.

Review the tactics that buyers often use against salespeople brought out in Chapter 2. Be ready with a satisfactory response when you recognize any of these tactics during the sales negotiation.

Establish Negotiation Guidelines Before the Meeting

We have emphasized the importance of going into the sales negotiation fully prepared so there will be a minimum of surprises from the buyer and so that any offers or concessions will have been evaluated as to their impact on the profitability of the sale.

Obviously, perfect planning against all eventualities is rare. But it is equally obvious that thoughtful planning ahead of the meeting with the buyer can prevent mistakes in judgement that can occur during any negotiation process.

Review your power advantages as discussed in Chapter 3 and the strategies and tactics suggested in Chapter 4. Be ready to cope with the tactics buyers may try as listed in Chapter 2.

Make a checklist of the points you want to consider, particularly with the more important prospects. Here are some suggestions you may want to consider.

Your answers to the questions will obviously be easier to make after you have covered the remaining Chapters, so don't be too concerned with them yet.

Your Negotiation Planning Checklist

1. What do you know about the prospect's needs, wants and problems that can be resolved by your proposal?

2. What power advantages do you have going into the sales negotiation?

3. What will be your first proposal on price and conditions? Is it high enough? Is it realistic? Does it give room for concessions if needed?

4. What are the benefits you will bring out that justifies this price if it is higher than that of the current supplier or your competition? These are the product and service benefits you normally bring out in your sales presentation except that they are tailored to what you have learned about the specific prospect.

5. What concessions can you make in price? What is the order in which they can be given, keeping in mind the principle of small increments.

6. When making each concession, what will you ask the buyer for in return?

7. What is your "bottom line" for price? For services?

8. What non-price concessions are you prepared to offer if needed? See list in Chapter 9 for suggestions.

9. Are you prepared for the negotiation tactics the buyer may try on you? Do you know how you will cope with them? Review Chapter 2 for suggestions.

10. Based on your estimate of the power balance between yourself and the buyer, do you have a negotiation strategy worked out? Review Chapter 4 for suggestions.

There are more checklists in the remaining Chapters of this book that will help make your planning for the sales negotiation more effective. While they are part of the Chapter devoted to a specific stage of the sale, like making the Presentation, they are considered during the Planning stage where the preparation for the sales negotiation is done.

Don't feel you need to write out answers to checklists like these for every sales call. A reminder is often all that is necessary. Refer to the checklists more often at first to make sure you're not overlooking something you should prepare for.

As you get more experience, a quick run through your own personalized checklist may be sufficient for all but the most important sales negotiation calls. Remember, however, that overlooking some factor on your checklist before going before a prospect could make the difference between making a sale and losing it.

Watch Out For False Assumptions

Salespeople have to make assumptions about the prospect's situation, motivations and probable decisions. We try to go into sales negotiations with as much knowledge as possible about the buyer, but lacking all that is needed, we end up with making assumptions or educated guesses. It is important, however, that these assumptions be on the up side rather than defeatist.

It's safer to make your presentation and suggestions based on a positive appraisal of the prospect's potential. Don't downgrade your expectations until you check them out through questions and observation during the sales presentation.

False assumptions on the downside lead salespeople to start the presentation and negotiation with proposals that are too low and to make concessions too early. Too many salespeople have gone into a sales negotiation thinking, "They can't afford to buy all that equipment so I'll open with the less expensive alternative." Later they often find that a competitor didn't make that assumption and ended up selling the same prospect the top quality equipment.

You have to make assumptions about most prospects, but don't trust them until you check them out during the sales presentation and negotiations.

Start with high expectations rather than low ones and modify them downward only when the evidence collected shows that you should.

The Expectation Factor in Negotiation

There have been a number of studies on negotiating to determine the personal characteristics of the negotiators who win or lose most often. The expectation level of the participants seems to have a direct bearing on what each was willing to settle for in the negotiation. The higher the expectations, goals or objectives, the higher the gains on the average.

The party who doesn't expect to get much out of the negotiations usually doesn't, even when the balance of power is in his or her favor. The party who sets high goals and has a commitment to strive for them, usually comes out better in the negotiations.

The expectation level of a salesperson entering a sales negotiation will have a decided bearing on its outcome. "Oh, I'll make the call, but I don't expect to make a sale to that company. Too much competition. Besides, our prices are too high." With this kind of attitude, there's little going for the success of the call.

With careful prospecting and qualifying effort, plus effective planning for the sales call, the sales negotiator should be able to meet the buyer with a high expectation level that will carry him or her to more successful negotiations and more profitable sales.

Who is In Control of the Sales Negotiation?

It is a principle of successful selling that the salesperson must be in control of the agenda. The person who controls the agenda controls what will be presented, what will be discussed and the timetable for the negotiation.

It is obviously easier for the buyers to control the agenda if they have the balance of power and want to exercise it. The buyers have control of the button which can terminate the session at will if the agenda fails to stimulate enough interest to keep it going to a satisfactory conclusion.

Salespeople CAN control the agenda, however, through pre-planning the steps to take, the benefits to stress, the strategies and tactics to use and a determination to keep the discussion on track. Whether or not this pre-planning and preparation will succeed certainly depends on the needs, desires and style of the buyer.

But one thing is sure, the salesperson will NOT control the agenda without such preparation and reasonable negotiation skills.

Make a Sales Negotiation Planning Worksheet

Successful salespeople plan their sales call carefully before facing each prospect or customer. Such planning avoids unnecessary surprises and helps make sure that the salesperson will cover all the essential facts and persuasion strategies necessary to make the call successful. The amount of planning they do for a specific call obviously depends on its importance and whether it is a new contact or part of a series of calls.

In our workshops on persuasive selling, we develop a model Planning Worksheet with the recommendation that the salespeople use it as a guide to preparing specific worksheets for each of the major sales calls.

At first, the inexperienced salesperson will want to spend more thought and time writing down the answers to the questions on the worksheet. With experience, just a few words will suffice to help the salesperson remember to get the needed information or apply the sales negotiation techniques most appropriate and at the right time.

The following sample Sales Negotiation Planning Worksheet will suggest items to include on your own Worksheet. You may not feel you need some of them. You may want to add others.

We suggest that you develop your own Worksheet and run off copies for about a month's anticipated calls. After that test run, you will probably have some changes to make.

SALES NEGOTIATION PLANNING WORKSHEET

Prospect: _____

Person to contact: _____

Objective of call: _____

1. What I need to know about the prospect's operation.

2. Prospect needs I may be able to satisfy.

3. Products (or services) I expect to suggest as solutions.

4. My first proposal on prices and conditions.

5. Opening remarks I plan to use to get attention and interest.

6. Questions I will use to identify the prospect's needs and to get more information on which to base a recommended solution.

7. Specific ways I plan to conduct the presentation.

8. What I expect to offer as a solution to a problem.

9. Benefits of this solution to the buyer personally and to the firm.

10. Questions I will ask to lead into each of the benefits.

11. Visual aids and proof material I plan to use in the presentation.

12. Third party experience stories and testimonials I plan to use.

13. Questions based on these stories and testimonials I will use.

14. Methods I will use to get the prospect to participate in the presentation.

15. Questions I will ask to probe the prospect's reaction to my presentation and to uncover additional needs.

16. Key points I will use in summarizing my proposal.

17. Possible resistance I anticipate and how I plan to overcome it.

18. Non-price concessions I will be prepared to offer if needed.

19. Price concessions I can make if needed and their order in small increments to the bottom line.

20. Concessions I will ask from the buyer in return for price and non-price concessions.

21. Negotiation tactics I anticipate from the buyer and how I will cope with them.

22. When and how I plan to lead into the close.

More Answers Are Coming

The Chapters which follow will provide specific selling and negotiating techniques and tactics to use in each of the stages of the sales negotiation starting with the Opening in Chapter 7. They will help provide your answers to the questions on the checklist and worksheet we suggested you make during the Planning stage.

But your best answers and results from your planning will come as you gain experience through watching your combined selling and negotiating skills work successfully.

7

Opening the Sales Negotiation

First Seconds Can Make Or Break the Sale

HOW YOU come through to the prospect in the first thirty seconds of your sales negotiation interview can be more important than anything you say or do in the next thirty minutes. In fact, if the prospect isn't properly impressed in these few seconds, you may not get the chance to remain for even the next three minutes!

Get to the Person With Authority to Negotiate

Sales negotiation success depends greatly upon getting to see and make a proposal to the person who has the authority to negotiate the purchase. Unfortunately, these important people often have a "castle guard" who go by such titles as receptionist, secretary or administrative assistant.

These people provide a screening function for the busy executives so they don't waste time with salespeople who have nothing to offer. But part of this same function is to let through anyone who has a legitimate reason for seeing the potential buyer.

So salespeople must have a strategy for providing the guards with a good reason for getting to see the key person, the one who can authorize the sale.

6 KEYS TO THE BUYING AUTHORITY'S CASTLE GATE

1. Get an appointment. A salesman in our group one day bragged that he could get in to see anyone in the world. There was the expected degree of skepticism about his ability to perform this amazing feat until he divulged his secret. "All I need," he said, "is for someone to get me an appointment."

If there is any sure way to get past the buyer's guard it is to have an appointment.

It's so comforting to be able to say "Yes, I do have an appointment," when the receptionist asks the inevitable question. Cold calls have to be made sometimes, but they waste time and energy. For selling involving a reasonable amount of negotiation, the sales call is usually made on the basis of an appointment.

Few prospects will refuse to grant a legitimate appointment at some future time.

Salespeople who use negotiation in their selling ask friends and enthusiastic customers for help in setting up appointments with the better prospects.

In some lines of business like insurance, appliances and office equipment, salespeople use staff people to set up appointments for them to save valuable face-to-face selling time. Where the firm doesn't have a staff for that purpose, some salespeople even hire someone at their own expense to make appointments with prospects. Increased sales more than pay the cost.

2. Have a confident manner. Whether you have an appointment or not, feel and demonstrate that you have a right to an interview. Show by bearing, appearance and voice that you expect to get in. Walk in briskly and with a smile and pleasant voice say, "Will you please tell Mr. Johnson that Mr. Walker from the Acme Corporation is here to see him?" Asking, "May I see Mr. Johnson," or "Is Mr. Johnson in?" only invites questions.

Confident salespeople inspire reciprocal confidence in the prospect that his or her needs can be satisfied properly. Positive confidence is important, but the fine line must be maintained between it and egotism or conceit which will irritate the prospect.

3. Promise a benefit. If you don't have an appointment, the guard may need a good reason to let you in, so he or she typically asks, "What do you wish to see him about?" This tells you that you must have a benefit to offer or the guard has been instructed to prevent entry in some fashion. Be prepared to show that your call will benefit the executive and not just your own desire. "I want to tell him about our delivery service" is YOUR benefit, not his.

A better approach might be, "I have some ideas that might save time and expense in his delivery operation. Will you please tell him I'm here?"

4. Be truthful. Telling the guard that your mission is very personal, confidential or highly important when it really isn't, may get you in once. But it will certainly keep you out the second time.

5. Be considerate. Be courteous, considerate and appreciative to the guard as well as others in the office. They make decisions, too. If you are rude and inconsiderate, they can slam the gate closed. If you show courtesy and understanding, they can make it easier for you to get in and even help you make the sale.

6. Don't let a turndown turn you off. All professional salespeople get turned away occasionally, but they don't give up easily. Try again. If you still can't get in, ask for an appointment that will get you in the next time.

Getting in to see the right person is not always easy. But seeing the wrong person wastes your time and effort. It's worth planning your strategy to increase your odds of getting in to see the people who have the authority to close the sale.

PLAN FOR THOSE FIRST FEW MOMENTS

Professional salespeople don't always agree on what tactics should be used during the first few minutes in front of the prospect. But all do agree on the importance of planning this important span of time. It is so important, in fact, that many texts give this stage in the sales call a special name, the Approach.

When they do, they frequently call all the planning that goes on after qualifying a prospect and before meeting the prospect face-to-face, the Pre-Approach. It matters little what you call it so long as you realize its importance and plan ahead for handling it properly.

Objectives For the First Moments of the Call

Salespeople have two important objectives for those few moments that begin their approach to the prospect. They are the first two mental steps we discussed in Chapter 6: To gain the prospect's favorable Attention, and to develop this Attention into positive Interest.

These are accomplished through the salesperson's appearance, actions and what he or she says . . . all equally important in these first critical moments.

Your physical approach to the prospect is over in a few seconds. It is the easiest step to accomplish, yet so many misjudge its importance and pay too little attention to it. It is in these first few seconds that your prospect makes those two important mental decisions we discussed in Chapter 6: "Shall I SEE this person?" and "Shall I LISTEN to him?" How the prospect answers these two questions determines whether or not the rest of your sales presentation stands a chance for success.

First Impressions are Visual

Your first impression on prospects during the sales interview is a visual one. If they are favorably impressed, they are more likely to want to listen to you. If not, everything you say or do must overcome a serious handicap in order to succeed.

If you come across like a rude or careless person, you will be treated like one.

Your appearance to prospects is a total of many things. It includes taste, cleanliness, attitude and general self-respect. It should be unnecessary to tell salespeople that they should be clean and well-groomed, yet many try to succeed without paying sufficient attention to these details.

With so many other problems to overcome in sales negotiation, why gamble away the chance on such an easily corrected distraction as an unkempt personal appearance?

With today's wide range of choices in clothing fashions, we will not attempt to suggest what salespeople should wear. They certainly have the RIGHT to wear whatever they please. By the same reasoning, however, the prospect has the right NOT to buy if the salesperson's attire offends him. Salespeople need to decide how their clothing choice for a sales call will affect the prospects.

For prospects in some types of selling, casual or high style attire might be preferred. For others, more conservative attire goes best. Experienced salespeople in your firm can give you guidance here. In selling as in other lines of work, the individual has to decide, "Which is more important, following my own preferences or compromising to increase my chances for success?"

During your approach to the prospect, your attitude must be one of confidence, just short of conceit. You must show confidence in your product or service, in your firm and in yourself.

Any lack of confidence as revealed in your manner, facial expression and speech is quickly relayed to the mind of the prospect. Confidence, while important, must not be carried to the negative extreme of boastfulness or egotism, of course.

11 Suggestions For Gaining Favorable First Impressions

The first objective of the approach, we have said, is to get the prospect's FAVORABLE attention. Anyone can gain attention with sarcasm, crude stunts or insults, but these do not create FAVORABLE attention. You have probably read stories of how salespeople landed sales with these kinds of tactics.

What you don't read about are the thousands of sales that were lost in the same way. Setting fire to the papers on prospects' desks would undoubtedly get their Attention and Interest quickly, but it probably wouldn't result in many sales for a pipe lighter salesperson.

Here are some simple suggestions used by successful salespeople to create favorable first impressions during the sales call. Give them a try.

1. *Dress neatly.* Lean to the conservative styles. They're safer.

2. *Be clean in dress and body.*

3. *Be confident in manner and bearing.* You came to help the prospects, not to beg from them.

4. *Be pleasant.* Talk with a smile.

5. *Have the prospects' names correct and pronounce them properly.* Check with someone before the interview if in doubt. Their names are among the prospects' favorite words. Use them.

6. *Leave your wraps outside if possible.* They're distracting.

7. *Don't apologize for taking the prospects' time.* They will be helped by your coming.

8. *Don't suggest that the call is unimportant or just made by chance.* Never say, "I was in your neighborhood and thought I would stop by." Make the call and the prospect important.

9. *Let the prospects start the handshake.* They might not like it. Practice a firm handshake, but avoid hurting the prospects. They won't think of you as strong and virile but rather as rude and thoughtless. Not a good start toward a sale!

10. *Sit down if possible.* If the prospect doesn't offer a chair, ask, "May I sit down?" As long as you stand, the prospect expects you will leave in a moment.

11. *Do not smoke.* This is not a moral issue. It just detracts from your presentation even where it doesn't actually antagonize the prospect. Isn't it worth waiting a few moments to get a sale?

15 TECHNIQUES FOR A SUCCESSFUL APPROACH

Here are some examples of different approaches used by salespeople to stimulate attention and interest. They are appropriate for either appointment or cold calls. Keep your mind open to ways you can use the ideas with changes to fit your selling situation and product or service.

1. Tell why you're there. Typical salespeople usually open the interview by identifying themselves with their own name and the name of their firm. If the first thirty seconds are the most important, salespeople waste half of them by giving the prospect these relatively unimportant facts first.

Professional salespeople who understand the importance of getting quick attention, start with the reason for their call first, like, "Mr. Foster, I want to explain a new method we have developed that may help you reduce your maintenance costs. I'm Charles Forbes of City Products Company."

If you have an appointment, you will naturally refer to your previous discussion on the telephone or the contents of the letter, telegram or mailgram.

2. Promise a benefit. Pick the strongest benefit (NOT a feature) of your product or service for the prospects and tell them what it is. "Mr. Carleton, I believe I have an idea that can save you time and labor costs on your welding operations." What can a prospect say but "How?" or "You'll have to prove that!"

It's easy to say "I'm not interested in hearing about a new welding torch." But it's not logical to say, "I'm not interested in saving time and labor costs."

3. Ask questions that lead to benefits. Questions make excellent openers if used properly. Some are worthless and time consuming, like "How's business?" The answer could ruin the whole presentation.

Use questions that make the prospects think about the needs they want to satisfy and the benefits they would like to have. For example, "Mr. Chalmers, if I could shorten your time in handling outgoing shipments, would you be interested?"

4. Ask questions to identify a problem. If you are using the problem-solving selling strategy described in Chapter 6, you can use questions during the opening of your sales call to identify a possible problem the prospect has that you might solve with your product or service. "How often do you have to get your carpets cleaned?"

If you suspected during your Prospecting stage that the prospect might have a particular problem, your questions can be structured to verify and quantify the problem. "How often do you have to call for service on your copying machine?"

The answers to these questions get the prospect to agree that there is or might be a problem and this arouses an interest for your presentation of a proposal to resolve the problem.

We will talk more about the use of questions during the opening of the sale later in this Chapter and cover the use of questions during the entire sales negotiation in Chapter 11.

5. Offer to make a survey. If appropriate to your selling situation, offer to make a survey to see if the prospects can benefit from your product or service. Make the point that the survey will not obligate them. "I have a machine that might reduce your wiring operations, but I'm not sure. With your permission, I would like to check a few things about your operation first and report back to you." Even when prospects might not allow the survey, they will be interested enough to want to hear more about your proposition.

6. Offer a trial. Although the trial is more frequently suggested later in the sales presentation when an immediate sale doesn't materialize, it might also be suggested in the approach in some instances. Business machines are frequently sold this way.

Offer to leave the product or a sample for the prospect to try out for a given period, then set up a date for the second interview.

7. Open with your product. If the appearance of your product will stimulate interest, use it to help open the interview. You might walk in with the product in your hands and put it on a desk or table then stand back.

If appropriate, you might ask a simple question like, "How do you like that?" Obviously the opportunities to use this opener are rare.

8. Be mysterious. If there is a element of mystery about the product, or a part of your product, exploit it by asking something like, "What would you say this is?"

9. Get the prospect into the act. Prospects can pretend to listen without actually doing so. But if you get them to physically participate in your opening, they can't think about anything else.

Get the prospects involved with their senses. Ask them to hold something, feel it, smell it, look into it, push some lever or button.

10. Use demonstration aids. Instead of actual products, visuals may have to be used in the approach as well as during the presentation. Visuals take a variety of forms, like photos, catalogs, models, cut-aways, charts, posters, photo slides, movies, videotapes, audiotapes, etc.

Ask permission to show them, like, "I think you might like to see a welding operation a firm like yours performs. May I show you three pictures?" "I have a five-minute slide presentation showing a new idea in merchandise display that I think would interest you. May I set it up here? Where is the nearest outlet?"

Make the benefit something other than just seeing your product.

11. Use a shocker. Open with a shocking statement of fact. Be sure you can back it up, of course. "All home videocassette players bought last year and before are now obsolete." Obviously that's because of a feature the salesperson's product now has but the prospect will want to know what it is.

12. Tell a story. Everyone likes to hear a story, if it's stimulating, short and told well. Collect them for use throughout your sales presentation. The story can be combined with many of the other approaches. For example, the salesperson produces a shattered pair of safety glasses for the "shocker" approach and then starts a story, "These glasses saved a worker's eye and saved a firm like yours a million dollar lawsuit. Let me tell you what happened."

A story about how one of your customers solved a problem with your product or service would be interesting to the right prospect. "Let me tell you how the Acme foundry solved a problem similar to yours last month."

13. Use a referral. Use the name of another firm or person as an introduction. "You are familiar with the ABC Company. Mr. Jones, the general manager, suggested that you might be interested in hearing about the installation we made for them."

Ask your customers routinely for referrals and use them.

14. Give something away. Some salespeople open the interview with a gift. The better types of gifts for this purpose direct the attention of the prospect to the salesperson's product or service rather than the gift itself. If the gift is a ballpen, for example, the salesperson might say, "I'd like to give you this pen with our compliments. On the side you'll note the words, 24-hour service."

15. Use a stunt. Here we include the thousands of stunts salespeople have used and will use to get the prospect's attention. While the better ones lead into the reason for the interview, they are strictly for attention. One salesperson tosses some coins in the wastebasket to illustrate wasting money. Another rolls dice on the prospect's desk to emphasize gambling with profits.

When you use a stunt, be very sure that it attracts FAVORABLE attention and doesn't antagonize the prospect instead. A hand tool salesperson could get attention by hammering a nail into the prospect's desk, but it's doubtful that the attention would develop into a sale.

After getting favorable attention, you must move quickly into stimulating the prospect's interest in satisfying a need or getting the benefit suggested by the stunt. "You may be losing money on your shipping operation every day without knowing it. May I ask you a few questions?"

HOW TO USE QUESTIONS FOR OPENERS

By using questions in the opening minutes of the sales interview, sales negotiators can accomplish several purposes vital to the outcome of the sale.

1. Questions help maintain the prospect's attention because one's mind can't wander too far when required to come up with answers to the questions.

2. When carefully selected and constructed, questions can be used to further qualify the prospect as having (or not having) a need that might be satisfied by the salesperson's product or service.

3. Once the need is established, the salesperson uses questions to clarify and quantify the need. Questions can also be used to see if the prospect recognizes the need, places any importance to it, and shows any interest in satisfying it. The answers to these questions will guide the salesperson in structuring the presentation phase and making the proposal.

4. In the problem-solving approach to selling discussed in Chapter 6, an extension of the need-satisfaction strategy, questions are used to uncover a problem the prospect might have and to get his or her agreement that it exists.

5. Questions in the opening phase of the sale, just as in the presentation, negotiation and closing phases, can be used to probe the prospect's feelings about current operations, possible problems with present suppliers, personal and company buying motives and preferences for the kinds of benefits the salesperson's product or service could provide.

Use a Worksheet to Plan Your Opening Questions

In selecting and wording opening questions, decide first what you must know about the prospect and the operation before you can make an intelligent proposal.

Many successful salespeople who use probing questions in opening the sales call, use a simple worksheet for that purpose. It need be no more than some notes on a pad of paper. It could be part of the total planning sheet shown in Chapter 6, or it could just pertain to the opening segment of your call.

After identifying the prospect at the top of the sheet, here are some headings you might use. We will discuss their purpose and use some examples. You will want to leave enough room between the headings for writing in the data, of course.

Objective of the call:
Attention-getter question or action I will use:
Information I will need to tailor my presentation:
Questions I will ask to get this information:
Information that I want the prospect to know:
Questions I will ask to make the prospect interested in hearing about that information:

Start with the specific objective for your call followed by an attention-getter question or action to open the call.

For example, let's assume your call objective was to get the personnel manager to use your temporary employee service. Your attention-getter might be to ask what kinds of problems she has in finding employees on an emergency, temporary basis.

If you want more information on the prospect's needs and problems, write down the specific information you want followed by the questions you will ask the prospect to get it.

For example, suppose you sell office copiers. You might want to know what copier is currently being used, how much use is made of it, what kind of work is done on it, and what problems the prospect is experiencing with the present equipment and supplier. You would write each of these information needs on your worksheet followed by questions you would ask the prospect to get the information you want.

There usually are some special features of your product or your service that you want to present early. Write these on your worksheet followed by set-up questions which are designed to make the prospect interested in listening to what you will say about the feature and its benefits.

For example, suppose you sell printing and your company prides itself on its ability to get the jobs out fast. You might write down questions like, "How often do you need printing done in a hurry?" or "What has been your experience in getting some printing you needed in a hurry?"

Preparing a worksheet might seem like too much work to do before making every call, and it probably is. We suggest you just try making one for your next important call as a test. The same worksheet will probably work for most of your routine calls on prospects from then on, subject to additions and improvements you will make from experience in planning what you will do and ask the prospects.

If you get a new product or add a new service or just think up new approaches, you can take a few minutes to write out a new or revised worksheet.

Whatever you do to plan ahead for that important few minutes when you open your sales call is bound to increase your chances of staying around long enough to get into the sales negotiation.

Sample Opening Questions

Here are sample questions for openers that will suggest some you could develop for your own opening moments. Start with the purpose of your call and the information you need.

"What brand of (your generic product) are you selling now?"

"How many office employees do you have?"

"What is your biggest problem with your present copying machine?"

"What are some of the problems you are having in getting service on your computers"

"What do you like most about (product now being used)?"

Ask Permission to Ask Questions

Most successful salespeople feel it is best to first ask permission to ask some questions. It is seldom refused. For example, the salesperson might say, "I think I may have some ideas you can use in your warehousing operation, Mr. Johnson, but I want to make sure. Do you mind if I ask you a few questions about your present procedure?" Few prospects will refuse to answer questions when put in this manner. After all, most of us like to hear of new ideas, especially when under no obligation to buy.

After getting permission to ask questions, the salesperson could make further explanation if necessary then ask questions to get the needed facts. "We have been able to save considerable warehousing costs for firms like yours, but I'm not sure how our equipment would work for you." Then he asks questions that will qualify the prospect's need like, "How large is your warehouse in square feet?" "What make of forklift are you using now?"

Don't Come On Too Strong!

Some salespeople make the mistake of coming on too strong when asking questions of the buyer. Some even feel that a measure of intimidation will get better results. Actually, the typical buyer seldom refuses to answer questions when presented in a friendly manner. But buyers will fight back at the feeling of being pressured and will hold back useful information about present conditions or needs. If the resentment is too deep, the buyer may flatly say, "It's none of your business!"

A more effective method for getting the needed information from the prospect is to be friendly, almost humble.

The reason for asking for the information must be made clear to the prospects: so you can be more helpful to them. It should never be implied that the information is needed just to make a sale for the salesperson, like, "We're pushing garden tools this month. How's your present inventory?"

More Help Coming On Ways to Use Questions

We will cover the use of questions in all phases of sales negotiation more fully in Chapter 11. In Chapter 12, we cover Listening, an important companion skill when asking probing questions. A good question loses its value if you don't listen properly to the customer's answer.

Plan Your Opening to Close More Sales

Plan ahead for what you will say and do in those important first few moments when you face the prospect in person for the first time. Check your present approach methods. Can they be improved? Do you want to try some of the suggestions described here with modifications to fit your product or service? What are other salespeople from your company doing that seems to work well?

When you have an approach that works well, you have increased your chances for continuing through to a successful sales negotiation.

8

Making a Persuasive Sales Presentation

Gateway To the Sales Negotiation

THE SALES presentation is the gateway to sales negotiations. Without it there is nothing to negotiate. The salesperson may have some activity requiring modest negotiating techniques early in the sales development stages, like getting the prospect to grant an interview.

But the real negotiating skills don't come into full play until after the initial sales presentation to the prospect or customer.

The negotiation session which finally results in the sale might not have opened with a complete sales presentation. That may have occurred days or even months before the final negotiations.

But the negotiation is still based on an effective presentation by the same or different salespeople that developed the prospect into a potential customer.

If the salesperson does a good job of opening the sale and making a persuasive presentation of the product or service, the prospect watches and listens attentively and forms an opinion on the potential purchase.

Questions and answers by both the salesperson and the prospect during the sales presentation keep it moving toward its objective . . . to communicate the proposition and to identify the features and benefits of purchase.

DEVELOP YOUR OWN PRESENTATION PLAN

Much has been written and said in sales workshops and seminars on how to make an effective sales presentation. Whole books and seminars are devoted to this single subject alone.

In recent years, for example, salespeople were encouraged to psycho-analyze their prospects and customers, give them a personality identification, then select a sales procedure designed to lead that type of individual to buy. We will take no stand on any of the many systems except to suggest that you listen to them and develop the methods that seem to work best for you.

There seems to be a trend "back to the basics" in selling, however, and fortunately that fits into our desire here to use the most popular basic formula simply as a means for illustrating how selling through negotiation works.

If we succeed in helping you integrate the best techniques of basic negotiation into our basic selling formula, you will have little trouble in integrating your new negotiation skills into any selling method you prefer. So let's continue with the basic selling plan outlined in Chapter 6.

Convert Interest into Desire

In Chapter 7, we said that in the first few moments before the prospect, the Approach, the salesperson has to get his or her favorable Attention and arouse Interest in learning more about the product or service.

The purpose of the Presentation is to convert this simple Interest into a Desire to own the product or service or to go along with a proposition the salesperson proposes.

There is a big difference between interest in a product and the desire to own it. The visitor to the zoo can become quite interested in an elephant without wanting to own it. Your prospect might be quite interested in your product, how it works, what it will do. He might be so interested that he will tell his friends all about the amazing new product. But he will not buy it or even negotiate for it until you first make him aware that he NEEDS it and then make him WANT it! And that calls for an effective sales presentation.

In looking back over your personal purchases, you can agree that you never bought anything until you determined first that you NEEDED it. No matter how great the bargain was, you first had to mentally determine that you needed the product or service. Sure, we all look at some of the things we possess and wonder why in the world we ever bought them. I mentioned earlier that I own an African drum made out of a hyena skin. Today I wonder why I bought it, but when I did, it satisfied a need. I keep it as an example of the power of need satisfaction in selling when discussing presentations with salespeople.

At the time I bought the drum, and at the time you bought ANYTHING you own, we had a basic need that those items satisfied sufficiently to make us part with our money to buy them.

If you look back at those basic buying motives identified in Chapter 5, at least one of them was strong enough at the moment, perhaps amplified by a good sales presentation, to make us buy.

Establish the Prospect's Need

We discussed the five basic mental steps a buyer must take in buying anything in Chapter 6. The third step was Conviction, the determination by the buyer that he or she has a need for the product or service the salesperson offers.

Conviction was inserted into the famous AIDA selling formula (Attention-Interest-Desire-Action) some years ago when it became apparent through studies that people had to be convinced they had a need for something before they desired it enough to buy it. This led to the Needs Satisfaction approach to selling that is popular today.

Salespeople consciously using the Needs Satisfaction approach, use the prospect's need as the starting point for the sales presentation. The salesperson determines the prospect's need before the call or through questions early in the call, then gets the prospect's agreement that the need exists.

For the remainder of the presentation, the salesperson attempts to convince the prospect that his or her product or service is the best solution to the established need.

The Problem-solving Approach discussed in Chapter 6 is just an extension of the Need-satisfaction idea. If the need is the resolution of a problem, the salesperson helps the customer evaluate the relative advantages and disadvantages of the alternative solutions.

This takes more of the salesperson's time than simply identifying a need, but the problem-solving approach builds up a consultant-client relationship with customers. It is typically found in industrial selling of technical products and services.

Probe for Needs that Match Your Solutions

The professional salesperson typically opens the sales negotiations call by asking the prospect some probing questions to establish the need for the salesperson's product or service.

The salesperson starts off with a fairly low key statement like, "Mr. Johnson, the reason for my call is that I have some ideas which might reduce the cost of your word processing operations. Do you mind if I ask you a few questions?"

Prospects are normally interested in ideas that will improve their situation, so they seldom refuse to answer the questions. The probing questions that follow must be carefully structured to give the desired information on which to build the presentation.

We discussed these probing questions in Chapter 7 as important for establishing and quantifying the need and getting the prospect's agreement that the need exists. Probing questions are also needed in the problem-solving selling strategy to establish the problem the salesperson hopes to solve.

The probing questions early in the sales presentation give the salesperson an overview of the current situation such as the amount of the product now used, the current supplier, preferences, and any problems with the product or supplier.

Knowing these facts about the current operation and the attitudes of the buyer gives the salesperson suggestions on what approach to take in the remainder of the sales presentation and the features and benefits that will probably appeal most to the prospect.

Sample Questions for Establishing Needs

In addition to the sample questions given in Chapter 7, here are examples of questions whose answers will help guide the remainder of the sales presentation. Keep in mind how the answers will help the salesperson structure the presentation.

"How many employees do you have in your word processing department?"

"What brand of (your generic product) do you use?"

"What brand of (your generic product) sells best for you?"

"Who is your present supplier of (your generic product)?"

"What are some problems you are having with your present (your generic product)?"

"What do you like most about your present system?"

"How do you feel about the service you are getting from your present supplier?"

"What are your critical concerns when you purchase (your generic product)?

Start the Sales Negotiations High

Start the sales negotiation presentation with as many factors in your favor as possible. Now and then we hear of salespeople opening their presentations with something like, "Now before we get started, Mr. Folger, I want you to know that we are prepared to give you 10% off our regular price and next day delivery." Is there any question on where the concessions will probably start?

If the salesperson knows about a need for high quality or an exclusive feature or special delivery accomodations, these should be factored into the initial proposal presentation.

The smart buyer will refrain from mentioning any pressing needs until after the initial presentation. Buyers know that the best time to mention special requirements is after the salesperson has set a price or better yet, made a price concession. The buyer figures that rather than lose the sale, the salesperson will absorb the added conditions.

Be prepared for these contingencies in the early stages of the sales negotiation and allow room for them.

Use Questions to Guide Prospect Decisions

The professional salesperson uses carefully planned questions during the presentation to gather information that will guide the salesperson on which tactics to use in the negotiating and closing stages.

The questions can be used to determine the prospect's reaction to the features and benefits of the product or proposal. For example, the salesperson might ask about a key feature, "How do you feel about being able to switch from standard to legal paper and back just by pushing a button?" The buyer is expected to say, "That would sure save a lot of time!"

Using a question got an answer that shows the degree of the prospect's interest in the feature and in the benefit of saving time.

Probing questions can also be used to help the prospect make minor decisions as the presentation progresses that can be referred to by the salesperson during the negotiation to remind the prospect of the commitment and to encourage the right decisions.

For example, the salesperson might ask during the demonstration, "Do you feel that this automatic adjustment feature would speed up your operation?" The prospect says, "It sure would." "What effect would that have on your labor costs?" "Well, it should reduce them somewhat."

Later during the closing or negotiation phase, the salesperson can refer to this commitment by the prospect. "During the demonstration, you said that the time savings resulting from the automatic adjustment feature of this equipment would result in reducing your labor costs. Could you make an estimate on how long it would take to completely return your investment in this new equipment on labor savings alone?"

The prospect's answers and reactions during the sales presentation are valuable tools for laying the groundwork for the sales negotiations. Plan your presentation so that it provides this added power for you in the negotiation and closing stages.

A little later we will show how questions can be used during a product demonstration. In Chapter 11, we will discuss the questioning techniques in more detail.

Try to Close the Sale Early

At the end of your initial sales presentation, try to close the sale. Experts call this the Trial Close and we will cover that in Chapter 10. If the prospect buys at this point, wonderful!

The only negotiations needed from that point on will be simple agreements on things like time of delivery or method of payment.

But when the prospect hesitates or refuses to buy after the presentation, questions the benefits or rejects the price, the salesperson has to turn to the negotiation strategies and tactics for handling customer resistance. We will discuss these in Chapter 9.

CONVICTION REQUIRES PROOF

A prospect may recognize a need and have the desire to satisfy that need and still not buy. While there are a variety of reasons for this reluctance, fear of making the wrong decision is a powerful one. It's the job of the salesperson to determine what the uncertainty is and then to assure the prospect that buying his or her product or service will be the right decision.

Just telling the prospect, "You can't go wrong with this product," might work now and then with prospects who have almost made up their mind and trust your judgement from past experience.

But the majority of prospects are skeptical of claims and will insist on proof for those claims that will influence their decision. So successful salespeople develop and maintain a collection of "proof devices" for those key benefits which experience shows the customers rely on most.

4 Basic Types of Proof

There are many ways to prove your benefit claims during your presentation or during the negotiation phase, but most of them could be classified into these four basic categories.

1. Physical proof. Here you prove the benefits by letting the prospect experience the features first hand that will provide them. Show him the braces that make the product stronger; let her feel the softer fabric; let them listen to quiet operation.

Where the product itself cannot be demonstrated, photos and a variety of audio-visual aids can be used to provide the physical experience.

Mentioning or showing a copy of a guarantee helps overcome fear of making a wrong decision on those factors covered by the guarantee.

2. Testimonials. Stories of how another person or firm used the product or service successfully is proof second in value only to the prospect's own experience. A testimonial letter may be shown with the story for even stronger proof. If the customer is known by the prospect, the proof is even stronger. The stories can be woven into the sales presentation or used later to overcome resistance and build assurance for making the right decison.

3. Expert opinion. The salesperson tells what experts have said about the product or service. This may be the report of a recognized testing laboratory, an article in a magazine, a news story or a comment by a recognized leader in the business or community.

4. Logical argument. The decision to buy can obviously be made only by the prospect. But the salesperson can help the prospect think logically to help him or her come to the right buying decision.

The business equipment salesperson first gets agreement that a new machine will speed up certain kinds of operations. By using the prospect's own figures of salaries, space rental and other costs, the salesperson helps the prospect figure out that the new equipment will pay for itself in X-months from savings alone.

Logical proof is made more believable when the prospect participates in its determination.

MAKING THE DEMONSTRATION

The demonstration is the power tool of the sales presentation. The salesperson has obtained the prospect's Attention and has aroused some degree of Interest in the product or service during the Approach. Now the salesperson needs to convince the prospect that he or she can use the benefits the product or service offers and prove that they will be realized.

The professional salesperson practices on a good demonstration to assure that it is the best one possible. Many companies spend considerable time and money experimenting with demonstration techniques and aids which they can pass along to their sales staff.

Take advantage of all the research involved if this help is available from your company. Give their recommended demonstration technique a fair trial.

Once you have perfected a demonstration procedure that seems to produce results, do not change it unless you are convinced that the revision will produce even better results. Do not change it simply because you become tired of the routine. Slighting some points you normally give may cost you lost sales.

Remember that those prospects who haven't witnessed your demonstration yet will be just as interested as the first prospects who saw it.

4 Steps to Successful Demonstrations

The full sales demonstration is made up of a total of several smaller demonstrations that focus on simple features. Master each step and the full demonstration falls into place.

The full demonstration is composed of four basic steps. Let's analyze each one.

Step 1. Say something. What you say and how you say it during the demonstration is obviously most important to the outcome of the sale. Here are some hints from professional salespeople that might help you improve your sales talk.

a. Be enthusiastic. Your prospect will seldom have any more enthusiasm for your product than you do. If you are just lukewarm in your presentation, the prospect will not be as impressed as if you were enthusiastic. Enthusiasm is catching, but not nearly as much as the lack of it.

b. Don't make a speech. Use your conversational tone. Do not recite a prepared speech. Try to draw the prospects into the conversation with questions to get their opinion and reactions. Their reactions may clear up misunderstandings and help you locate the more important benefits.

c. Talk slowly. Without realizing it, we tend to talk faster and faster as we become more familiar with a product and give the same demonstration a few times. We may even begin to leave out details that seem insignificant. These details that might be missed by the prospects when the salesperson tries to hurry could contain the key to their understanding and appreciation of the product or service. Assume that the prospect knows nothing about it until you are convinced otherwise.

d. Tell and show. Key your words with your actions. Prepare your prospects so they focus their attention on what you are doing. The machine salesperson might say, for example, "I'm going to demonstrate how easy it is to reduce or enlarge your copies. First you press this button . . . "

Step 2. Do something. Here are five suggestions professional salespeople give to make the action portion of your demonstration more successful.

a. Take your time. Don't rush your demonstration. The very points which you omit or which you give too hurriedly might be the very ones that would clinch the sale.

After you have given your demonstration a few times, you will become so good at it that you can probably speed it up considerably. Don't do it! Keep it going at a pace that the prospect can follow. Repeat if necessary to make a point. Review those features and benefits which seemed particularly important to the prospect.

b. Maintain your enthusiasm. After you have given the same demonstration several times, you will get the same feeling one gets after seeing the same movie a fourth time. This could dull your enthusiasm and this is highly contagious for the prospect.

Remember that your prospect is seeing your performance for the first time. Make it good!

c. Put the prospect's attention where you want it. Don't let the prospects wonder what you're talking about. Don't let their minds move away to other things. Tell them to do something, like hold a paper, move a lever, turn a crank. If there is nothing to do, tell them what to look at, like, "Watch what happens when I pull this lever."

d. Make it look easy. If your product requires assembly or operation, it is important that you make it look easy to do. This is particularly true if you stress simplicity as a feature. Practice each element of your demonstration until you can do it smoothly and easily.

Prospects expect you to be an expert. If you can't operate the equipment, what chance would they have?

e. Don't fumble. Making the operation look easy includes avoiding fumbling if possible. This disturbs the prospect's attention and causes annoyance. Be sure that all the parts are on hand, all the items you plan to show. Know where they are so you don't have to waste time in front of the prospect looking for them.

A carefully planned and practiced demonstration is the best cure for "fumbleitis."

Step 3. Get the prospect into the act. There is no better way of getting and maintaining the prospects' attention than to get them to participate in the demonstration. You want them to feel that they already own the product. In doing so, you increase the chances of their remembering the selling features and benefits your product offers.

Professional salespeople recommend these points to watch in getting the prospects' participation.

a. Have them do something reasonably simple. Stay away from the more complicated jobs. You want the prospects to be able to do the thing you ask, easily and without embarassment.

b. Have them work an exclusive feature. You want the prospects to recognize and remember your product's superior features and benefits. This is part of the value of getting them to participate in the demonstration. Make a list of your exclusive and outstanding features. Select the ones that could be used to involve the prospects during your demonstrations.

c. Have them do something they would do often if they bought the product. If the prospects do something during the demonstration that they would do often if they owned the product, they experience the advantages and benefits. They mentally experience ownership and tend to resist having it taken away from them.

Obviously buying your product is the ideal solution to avoid having this happen!

Step 4. Ask questions. During the demonstration, ask questions to check on the effectiveness of your demonstration; to move the demonstration along and to get the prospect into an agreeable mood.

Use questions to locate the features and benefits which best fit the prospect's interests. "How important to you is the ease of selecting paper size?"

Use questions to get the prospect to make a commitment. "Do you feel that this higher speed would reduce your problem of people waiting for their copies?" Recall these commitments later during the negotiation stage as well.

Ask questions after you have made a point in the demonstration to see if the prospects understand the benefit and whether or not they would desire it. If they unquestionably understand the feature and its benefits, go on to your next demonstration point.

Use questions that call for an affirmative rather than a negative answer from the prospects. Experts say this creates a more positive mood in the prospect. Compare these two questions. "This isn't hard to operate, is it?" "Isn't this easy to operate?" While they cover the same point, the latter question is better because it calls for an affirmative answer.

Use questions that get the prospect to put his opinion in his own words. Compare these questions. "Wouldn't you like to have a brighter picture on your television set?" "How do you feel about having a brighter picture on a television set you own?"

The first question obviously calls for a yes answer, so the prospect gives it without really thinking.

When you ask prospects what they think, they are forced to consider the feature or benefit before giving you an answer. This implants the benefits more firmly in their minds. Even if their answer is negative, it gives you an idea of what they really want so you can bring out additional information or make a new approach.

Questions can be used during the demonstration to set the stage for the negotiations and closing the sale. When the prospects make a commitment in answer to a question, they actually make a small agreement that the product will answer their need.

Little questions lead to little agreements. Little agreements add up to the one big one . . . the final sale!

Chapter 11 demonstrates more uses for questions and techniques for using them profitably during the sales presentation.

Watch For Clues On Buyer Reactions

Watching for clues and interpreting them correctly helps you know how the sale is progressing.

If the clues are favorable, you can continue on your presentation plan. If not, you can make the changes or probe to find out where the difficulty is.

Observing the behavioral clues the prospect provides during the presentation stage can provide valuable information that can be used later during the negotiation stages. If price, quality, service or other factors find favor or resistance, the clues help tell the salesperson where the importance seems to lie.

Check Body Language, Too

Buyer clues come from what they say and their physical behavior, commonly called "body language." Since most buyers hold back on volunteer comments, salespeople have to use questions to uncover most of the verbal clues.

Simple observation of the buyer's body language provides clues as to the degree of interest of the buyer to the proposition and any antagonisms.

Chapter 12 gives suggestions for listening to the prospect's body language and how to interpret its signals.

Help the Prospect Make the Right Decisions

In Chapter 6, we listed the eight questions every prospect asks mentally before deciding whether to buy or not to buy. Since every one of the questions has to be answered yes before a sale can be made, it is important that the salesperson develop and conduct the sales presentation in a way that encourages the prospect to answer each decision favorably.

Some of these mental questions may not be answered to the satisfaction of the prospect until the Negotiation and Closing phases of the sale, but the salesperson increases the odds that they will by providing the answers effectively during the Presentation.

Some of the decisions will be made before the salesperson makes the call, depending upon how much the prospect knows about the needs, the product and the salesperson's firm. The salesperson has to determine early which decisions have been made and what the answer was. Those that were negative decisions must be changed to positive answers or the salesperson will be wasting his or her time on the sales call. There's no need to waste time on the decisions that are already favorable except to strengthen them.

How to Help the Prospect Decide in Your Favor

Let's consider the eight mental decisions again and link them to the sales presentation. Review the suggestions discussed in this section for sales presentations as needed.

1. *Will I SEE this person?* The fact that you are in front of the prospect, ready to make the presentation, shows that this decision was favorable.

2. *Will I LISTEN him/her?* Get the prospect's favorable attention and interest. Ask questions to stimulate this interest and to open the way to isolating needs associated with your product or service.

3. *Do I NEED the benefits offered?* Establish the need through observation and questioning. Make the prospect aware that the need exists and get agreement that it would be desirable to have it satisfied.

4. *Will the PRODUCT/SERVICE offered give me these benefits?* Appeal to the prospect's buying motives. Select those benefits that lead to the prospect's conviction that your product or service satisfies the need. Offer proof that the benefits will be obtained.

5. *Is this person the BEST SOURCE for the product/service?* Establish the reasons why the prospect should buy from you rather than a competitor. Point out service, convenience, reliability of the manufacturer, your firm and yourself. Compare total cost including these advantages and benefits.

6. *Is the PRICE reasonable?* Convince the prospect that your total price is fair for all the benefits obtained. This does not necessarily mean the lowest price obtainable. Repeat the benefits that offset price.

Resell the benefits that might not be understood or appreciated. Should the prospect show a willingness to take fewer benefits at a lower price, be ready to negotiate.

7. *SHOULD I buy?* Ask for the order to start this decision. If there is hesitation, be prepared to resell the benefits that seemed to appeal most to the prospect during your presentation.

8. *Should I buy NOW?* This decision follows the previous one, of course, and the strategy for getting the prospect to buy now is to emphasize the benefits that can start now with buying and the losses that would occur every day the prospect waits.

After the Trial Close

A successful sales presentation sets the stage for closing the sale. Professional salespeople use trial closes at strategic points during the presentation to check on the prospect's desire for the product or service and to uncover any resistance that can be resolved.

If the trial close results in the sale, so much the better. Time is saved that can be invested in other sales calls.

Unfortunately, not all presentations, even the best ones, end in a sale. If the sale is not made at the end of the presentation, the salesperson has to enter the Negotiating Resistance and Closing stages to get yes answers on the last two buying decisions.

We will cover the strategies and tactics for these phases of the sale in the next two Chapters.

9

Handling Resistance in Sales Negotiation

I object!

ASK any professional salespeople to describe their favorite sale and it will usually go something like this, "I gave the prospect my usual presentation, told him the price, he said he'd take it and started writing out the check." Those are the sales we fondly remember because they happen so seldom. More often there is a period between the presentation and closing the sale where the prospect refuses to buy or raises objections to some portion of the proposition.

Too many salespeople worry about facing objections. They equate them with personal rejection by the prospect. But experienced salespeople, while not encouraging them, consider them opportunities for determining what must be done to complete the sale.

By objecting, the prospect is participating in the sale, providing a guidance system for tailoring the rest of your sales negotiation to the prospect's needs and desires.

The salesperson's skills in handling resistance and in negotiation strategy may have to be utilized during the Presentation if the buyer shows resistance early to parts of it, like certain features, or asks the price, or questions performance data.

But they are given their greatest test immediately following the Presentation when the salesperson asks the prospect for the order and is refused. Unless the prospect's resistance can be overcome or negotiated, there will be no sale!

WHERE DOES NEGOTIATION COME IN?

Since our emphasis in this book is selling more through the use of negotiation skills, we should get an understanding of the terms we will be using in this Chapter . . . handling resistance, overcoming objections and negotiating. While the desired end result is the same, to get the prospect to agree to buy, the strategy and tactics will vary somewhat depending on the form of the prospect's resistance to buying.

People who sell have had to cope with resistance to buying since the beginning of business history. In fact, without such resistance there would be no need for salespeople.

Those who were more successful in selling were those who were able to overcome customer objections through better communication of benefits and persuasion to satisfy needs. So those charged with the development of salespeople carried their training beyond the ability to make a good sales presentation. They added the important skills of coping with resistance and persuading people to buy.

In this Chapter we will review the basic techniques for overcoming buyer resistance and objections that professional salespeople find most effective. We will classify these as the objections prospects raise with the salesperson's original offer or proposal because they do not understand the benefits they would receive through buying the product or service, or for some reason they do not want to pay the price the salesperson asks.

In sales negotiation, in its broadest interpretation, the salesperson still utilizes his or her basic selling skills for handling resistance and overcoming objections. But in the stricter interpretation of sales negotiation, the salesperson does not begin to negotiate until he or she suggests changes in the original offer or proposal to meet the buyer's resistance and objections.

The salesperson first tries to overcome the buyer's resistance to the terms of the original offer or proposal and close the sale. Failing this, the salesperson then enters the negotiation phase where concessions or alterations to the original proposal are agreed upon, such as a lower price or added benefits.

Negotiation Requires Coping with Resistance

Salespeople have to utilize the same skills in persuasion and in handling resistance when they enter the negotiation stage as they did in presenting the original proposal. The buyer now has to be persuaded to accept the new proposal, and may have objections to it, too.

Both parties to most sales negotiations will have some resistance to proposals that are made. If there weren't any, there wouldn't be any need for negotiation to resolve the objections.

The difference between a sale and a no-sale in sales negotiations usually depends on how well the salesperson handles the buyer's resistance and objections.

We will discuss first the techniques successful salespeople use in handling resistance and overcoming objections in general. Then we will discuss negotiation techniques that can be used if concessions appear necessary.

Why Salespeople Welcome Objections

We all prefer the sales calls where the prospects raise no objections as long as they buy. It's when they refuse to buy that we welcome hearing what the objections are so we can use them as clues on what to do next to move the sale to a close.

The most difficult kind of prospect to sell is the one who sits there, pretends to listen to our story, acts pleasant, gives no resistance, but simply doesn't buy.

Man conquered air by using its resistance to lift the wings of a plane, not by fighting it. Professional salespeople conquer selling problems by using the prospect's objections rather than fighting them. They depend upon objections to point out those areas where the prospect needs more information, more convincing.

We don't suggest that you go out of your way to cause a prospect to raise objections. On the contrary, it's better to build the answers to expected objections into your presentation. But it is important to anticipate resistance and objections and to be prepared to handle them constructively through re-selling and negotiation.

3 Basic Types of Prospect Objections

We are all prospects for other salespeople from time to time, so we should understand why our own prospects raise objections and resist buying anything. Once professional salespeople determine the real reason the prospect is resisting, they can take steps to minimize the resistance or eliminate it entirely.

Most customer objections fall into these three basic categories:

1. The Sincere Objection. The prospects really mean what they say. With a sincere objection, prospects bring up those things they feel are real disadvantages in your product or service. Until you answer them satisfactorily, you should not try to close.

2. The Insincere Objection. The prospects do not mean what they say and are just expressing an objection to avoid making a buying decision or to get rid of the salesperson. It is just a stall rather than a true objection.

3. The Hidden Objection. The stated objection is not really the real one. A man may say he can't afford a new sports car when he really doesn't buy because he is afraid his wife will object to the style.

The salesperson must be able to distinguish the difference between a sincere objection and a stall because the skills required to handle each are different. It is difficult to separate the two because they may be expressed with the same words. When in doubt, it is better to assume that the objection is sincere and handle it accordingly.

Salespeople need to probe deeper to get to the hidden objection so they can handle it properly. Unless it is properly identified and reduced, the sale will be lost.

7 Reasons Why Prospects Raise Objections

Here are some beliefs prospects may have that cause them to raise objections or refuse to buy:

1. They genuinely do not need the product or service.
2. The product or service does not satisfy their recognized need.
3. The value of the product or service does not equal the price asked for it in their estimation.
4. They cannot afford to buy it. They may not have the funds or they may prefer to use the funds they have for other purposes they give higher priority.
5. They resist making changes in their current situation.
6. They want to wait while they compare other solutions and costs.
7. They are prejudiced against the product, the firm, the salesperson, the proposed solution.

Perhaps the most common objection given by prospects is, "The price is too high." This could fit into any of the three basic categories of objections. It could be entirely sincere; insincere and just a stall; or it could be used to cover up the real objection. We will discuss specific ways to cope with this type of objection later.

3 Steps in Handling Prospect Resistance

Let's discuss three important steps you must take to handle the resistance you face to some degree with every prospect. Taking one step without the others loses much if not all of the power you have available.

Step 1. Know the ANSWERS to the objections. Before you can handle objections, you must obviously know the answers. No amount of skill in techniques for handling resistance can make up for a lack of information about your product or service and the benefits it offers to your prospect.

Professional salespeople prepare themselves with answers by writing down the common objections they expect to get and adding others later as they meet them during their sales interviews. Once they have identified the possible objections, they write out their best possible answers for each one.

Some firms use sales meetings to collect common objections and have the salespeople as a group contribute suggested answers or solutions.

Step 2. Know the TECHNIQUES for applying the answers. When you write out the answer to an objection, it may be helpful to also write out your favorite technique for delivering it as well. For example, a salesperson might write for later use, "I understand how you might feel that way, (the technique of agreement) but the slightly heavier weight of our machine means that it can take more abuse and will save you money on repairs. (the answer)"

Step 3. Know WHEN to use the techniques. Knowing when to use a particular technique follows no particular rules. It involves an understanding of the prospects you face, their mood, their pressures, their previous attitudes. A technique that works on one prospect may not work on another. Expect to make mistakes, all professional salespeople do. But when you make a mistake, it means you have tried.

When you try to meet resistance with the right answer, the right techniques and with the right timing, your chances for overcoming the resistance and making the sale are greatly improved.

19 TECHNIQUES FOR HANDLING RESISTANCE

Here are nineteen basic techniques used by professional salespeople to meet and successfully overcome prospect resistance. Some overlap in principle but are listed separately because they use a different tactic. They are not in any particular order of importance. They all work together in the general strategy of using the prospect's objections to the salesperson's advantage in moving toward the successful completion of the sale.

1. Relax. When the prospect voices an objection, don't tense up like you want to fight or give the appearance that the objection frightens you. Just relax and give the appearance of thoughtful confidence.

2. Listen attentively. Let the prospects talk. Give them your full attention. Don't cut them off with counter objections or quick answers. You want to fully understand the objection; then you want the prospects to feel that you are sincerely interested in their opinions and their problems. As they hear themselves talk, their objections usually sound less and less important to them.

It's like letting the air pressure out of a balloon and watching it get smaller. If you interrupt, they will magnify their objections or defend them and fail to hear what you say.

3. Think before you answer. Take a little time, even though you might have the answer on the tip of your tongue. It's good strategy to think before you speak because you might come up with a better answer or technique.

But perhaps more important, you impress the prospects with your honest concern and avoid the atmosphere of high pressure selling.

4. Watch your temper. An unreasonable objection might upset you, but hold on. Letting the prospect know how stupid or untruthful you think he is may satisfy your ego, but it doesn't make sales. Regardless of how the objection affects you, don't let your words, voice or facial expression convey your feelings.

Watch that smile, too. It's safer to stay serious. Have you ever had someone smile at you in a way that clearly means they consider you not too smart?

If the other party becomes abusive, cut off the negotiations and leave without argument. The prospect may repent for his or her actions and invite you back. If you show the prospect up, you may never get another chance.

5. Handle the resistance at once. There will be situations where you would prefer to postpone your answer to an objection until you can bring out some features or benefits more forcefully.

Price questions, a type of objection, are a good example. Professional salespeople, however, recommend, "Meet the objection as soon as it is raised." This doesn't mean that you have to answer it fully, but you should at least acknowledge it.

When you say you will answer her objection later, the prospect keeps thinking about it and may not listen to what else you say or do. She may think you are avoiding the answer and lose confidence in you. Sometimes the lone objection may be the only obstacle to the sale. Handle it effectively and you speed up the close of the sale.

It's natural to want to postpone discussion of price until you have had time in your presentation to present the benefits that justify your price. Here are some examples of how the professional salesperson meets the price question and still postpones full consideration of it.

A prospect asks, "How much does it cost?" The salesperson replies, "The price is $465, but let's just write that amount down here and come back to it later after we talk about your present requirements." While the salesperson talks he or she writes down savings figures opposite the price to help minimize it.

A prospect says, "That looks pretty expensive. What does it cost?" If you have several models and prices, you can say, "The price depends on what model we think best answers your need. Let me first ask you a few questions."

6. Suggest, don't argue. Your attitude must be one of helpfulness. You want to cooperate with the prospects, not do battle with them. Few people are convinced by losing an argument. Professional salespeople sum it up with this philosophy, "Win an argument and lose a sale." By the use of persuasive suggestions, you can move the prospects to form the right conclusions for themselves.

7. The direct denial. This technique is rarely used because it has the danger of antagonizing the prospects. It is used only when the prospect tells an absolute falsehood which, if allowed to stand, would destroy the sale anyway. In this method, the salesperson emphatically denies the objection without being offensive. For example, a wholesaler prospect might say, "I understand that you are now selling direct to retailers." The salesperson might soften his denial like this, "Of course you don't mean that. I'm sure you know that we sell only through wholesalers."

8. Concede first. This might be called an "indirect denial" when compared to the previous technique. Here you concede or acknowledge that you understand your prospect's point of view, but you proceed to provide the information or proof that his view is wrong . . . in a nice way. The idea, of course, is to let the prospects down easy without embarassment or antagonism.

"Feel-Felt-Found" Method. Many salespeople like the "Feel-Felt-Found" method because these words are used in the typical concession. It goes like this, "I understand how you FEEL, Mr. Johnson. (I'm empathizing with you.) Mr. Walker over at National Industries FELT the same way at first. (You are not alone in feeling this way.) But he FOUND that after installing our system . . ." (Here is proof that you can get the same benefits.) This is also part of the technique of using third parties mentioned later.

9. Convert the objection into a question. Objections invite arguments but questions invite answers. Salespeople find that when they can convert the prospect's objection into a question, they can answer the question without proving the prospect wrong. We mentioned before that most objections are unanswered questions.

Here is an example of converting an objection into a question that can be answered. The prospect says, "We can't afford to switch to your copying equipment." Instead of saying, "You certainly can, and I'll prove it to you," the salesperson might say, "You raise a good question, Mr. Fowler. Would changing your present duplicating methods to our copying equipment save you more than the cost of the new installation. Is that the question?" If the prospect says no, you can get to the real question. If he says yes, you can proceed to answer the question. Always end the situation by asking, "Does that answer your QUESTION, Mr. Fowler?" Do not call it an OBJECTION!

If the objections are vague, they can often be cleared up by restating them in the form of questions. This tends to minimize rather than exaggerate the objection.

10. Offset the objection with benefits. When prospects have a valid objection, you can agree with them. But don't stop there. Outline the other benefits which offset the disadvantages. For example, you might say, "Yes, our unit will take a little more space than the one you're using now. But the heavier construction will save you repair and replacement costs."

11. Boomerang the objection into a benefit. Sometimes the objection can actually be turned around into a reason for buying. Here is an example. "I'm glad you mentioned the heavier weight, Mr. Briggs. We have strengthened the frame and mounting brackets and are using a heavier duty motor in this model. It does weigh a little more, but its heavier construction assures you of longer continued operation and less maintenance expense." Be careful to avoid the inference that the prospect should have understood the advantage. Give him credit for understanding it even though he didn't.

12. Probe for the real objection. The stated objections often hide the prospect's real objection. When they say, "Your price is too high," they usually mean, "My desire is too low." When this is the case, salespeople know they must present more benefits rather than argue for the price. Look behind the objection that is just a stall. Until you locate the real objection, you cannot overcome it and complete the sale.

13. Let third parties give the answer. When the salesperson and the prospect talk, they may come to verbal blows that settle nothing and may antagonize the prospect. Bringing in a neutral third party to give the answer softens the reply, makes it impersonal, more believable. You might say, "I understand how you feel, Mr. Keller. Bill Jones over at National Foods felt at first that the system might not work for him. But let me show you a letter he wrote us after using our system for a year." Now Bill Jones is giving the answer to the objection, not the salesperson who the prospect expects to be biased.

Keep a supply of references on tap for use in answering your anticipated objections.

14. Use the Echo response. Sometimes the response of the prospect doesn't give you enough information to make an intelligent answer. It often helps to "echo" or reflect the objection. For example, if the prospect says the price is too high, repeat the key words, "Too high?" This should stimulate more feedback and information, like, "Yes, it's more than we have budgeted." An alternative "echo" response that should get more information to work on is, "Why do you say that?"

15. Reduce the time frame of the problem. Reduce the problem to a short time denomination to make it appear more acceptable. The price is a common problem that can be treated this way. The prospect says, "$250 for a chair is more than I wanted to pay." The salesperson reduces the cost image to small time periods, like, "How long do you think you'll keep this beautifully constructed chair? At least twenty years, I'm sure. That means that it will cost you less than twenty-five cents a week to enjoy its beautiful styling and comfort. I'm sure that just the pride alone of owning this beautiful chair will be worth more than that to you, don't you agree?"

We will discuss additional ways to minimize the price objection later.

The same technique can be used to minimize objections other than price, like miles per gallon for an automobile. The prospect says "But this car gets only 27 miles per gallon and the other gets 30." The salesperson reduces this to weekly consumption difference something like this, "Yes, the ratings do make this difference. You said you drive about 15,000 miles a year, so that would be about a gallon a week. You have to decide whether you would rather have the (name the additional benefits) for the week or save a gallon of gas."

16. Override the shortcomings. When the objection is to an authentic shortcoming in your product or service, admit the shortcoming but stress the stronger benefits. "You're right, this equipment will not perform the X-job. But you said that it did the Y-job in which you are most interested in an outstanding fashion. It would be nice to have both, but your primary concern is doing the Y-job well, isn't it?" "Yes, I agree that the equipment is a little larger than the space you had planned for it. But I'm sure that the higher speed and the cost-saving benefits are worth more than the slight inconvenience of moving to another location, don't you agree?"

As in the previous technique, you can reduce the time frame for the shortcoming by asking the prospect, "How often would you use (the missing ingredient)?" If the prospect admitted he wouldn't use it very often, stress the benefits that will override the value of the occasional use.

17. Don't offend the prospect. Few persons enjoy having their opinion attacked or any action that reflects on their personal knowledge or ability. That's why it's easy for a salesperson to offend the prospects while trying to counter their resistance to buying. But the prospect's objections must be answered if a sale is to be made. Be careful in phrasing your answers so they don't imply that the prospect is stupid or is not telling the truth.

Here are some ways to take the edge off of your reply:

a. By taking the blame away from the prospect. You might say, "I'm sorry that I failed to make the point clear." or, "You're quite right in feeling the way you do now. But let me show you how another company like yours found they could save many hours of labor with this equipment.

b. By making a concession first. You might say, "Yes, the price is higher than you are paying now. But when you consider that you're getting additional (benefits) . . ." Another example, "Normally what you say is quite true, but with our service we have eliminated that problem."

c. By saying that other people feel the same way. Another way of conceding is to imply that other smart people felt the same way. "The superintendent at Universal Plumbing said the same thing at first. But let me show you a photo of his present installation that saved over seventy man-hours of labor the first week."

You can also use the Feel-Felt-Found formula for your replay which was described in Technique 8.

d. By paying tribute to the prospect's idea. You inflate the prospects' ego by giving them credit for their stand, like this, "I admire your concern with safety and I agree that this is an important factor. Let's see how our service can speed up your operation and yet be safe for the employees."

e. By blaming insufficient information. "I can understand how you might think that from your experience with similar products, but . . ." You can blame others, like "Your service people may not have given you all the facts." You can give another authority, "You're right, the first report did give that recommendation. But in the supplement here, they modified their stand because of additional data."

18. Sympathize. Disarm the prospects by sympathizing with their problem represented in the objection. It puts you on their side so you can work together to solve the problem, hopefully with your product or service.

For example, you might say, "I see what you mean. That does appear to be a problem. Let's see how we might work this out." When you show that you are fair-minded and are willing to consider their concern, the prospects will be more willing to hear more about how your product or service will resolve their problem or need.

19. Answer possible objections before they are raised. With a little experience in selling a new product or service, you become familiar with those objections that are raised over and over again.

You can forestall these objections by incorporating the answers into your sales presentation. You cannot eliminate all objections this way, of course, but you will get to the close of the sale quicker and easier when you can head off the more troublesome objections.

When you anticipate an objection, you will not be caught off guard by it when the prospect brings it up. You will gain the confidence of the prospects more surely when you can handle their objections smoothly, convincingly and without offending them.

Handling the "You-Gotta-Do-Better-Than-That" Tactic

Salespeople who sell a fairly uniform and highly competitive product are familiar with buyers who lean back in their chairs, put their hands behind their heads and say, "You gotta do better than that, my friend."

Inexperienced salespeople may take this to be just a friendly gesture on the part of the buyers, giving them information to help them make a sale by cutting the price. Unfortunately, it is a familiar negotiating tactic used by the professional buyers as brought out in Chapter 2.

Read again the discussion on handling the "gotta-do-better" tactic in Chapter 2. In review, the first defense is to know your price and how to defend it and we will discuss those techniques here.

If you eventually have to cut your price, be prepared to ask for concessions in return and especially a signed order immediately. "If I could meet that price, Mr. James, will you sign the order for five thousand units today?"

How to Handle the Price Objection

Professional salespeople are used to having prospects say, "Your price is too high." They don't like to hear it, of course, but they prepare strategies for handling the objection when it does come up.

There are a number of techniques to use and their choice depends upon the salesperson's interpretation of what the prospect really means by the statement.

It could be any of these:

a. "The price is more than I'm willing to part with to get the product."

b. "The price is really fair, but I just can't afford it."

c. "The price is higher than I would have to pay for the same thing elsewhere."

d. "I'll just say the price is too high to get rid of this person."

One successful salesperson said, "When my prospect says the price is too high, I hear him really say that his desire is too low. Then I go to work increasing his desire rather than arguing about the price."

The keys to overcoming the price objection are establishing the benefits to the prospect, creating more desire for them, and minimizing the price when compared to the benefits.

10 WAYS TO GET YOUR PRICE
BEFORE HAVING TO NEGOTIATE

Although price negotiation is probably the largest single activity in sales negotiation, professional salespeople try to overcome resistance to the original proposal price BEFORE resorting to negotiation. Here are some techniques to try to overcome price resistance before you negotiate a price concession.

1. Prepare for the price objection. While price is not the only objection you will face, it's the one you can most expect and prepare for. Be sure of your features and benefits, testimonials and proofs that will justify your price and provide persuasive counter-reasoning for the prospect.

2. Emphasize the benefits that justify the price. Your knowledge of competitive products as well as your own will help you emphasize the features, benefits and services during the presentation which outweigh the difference between your price and others.

Check after each benefit for the value the prospect places on it, "How would this affect your labor costs?" "Would you agree that this is top quality material?"

3. Consider price questions as buying signals. Asking the price is an indication that the prospect is somewhat interested in buying. It is actually a request for more information to help decide whether to buy or not. The prospect doesn't know what questions to ask to help make a buying decision, but does know that price is one of the factors, so he or she asks, "How much does it cost?"

Don't be timid or defensive when quoting a price or dealing with a price objection. Handle it confidently and tie it in with emotional buying motives. Prices are too high when salesmanship is too low.

4. Hold off on quoting price. Don't mention price until you have had a chance to stress the key features and benefits that will justify the price. Don't start with "Now this is our $699 model and this is the $849 model." If the prospect asks the price early in the presentation, give it but relate it to key features and benefits and continue, like, "This is the extra-large capacity model we sell for only $79.50. Let me show you how . . ."

If you have several price ranges, stall on giving the price, "The price will depend on which model will work best for you. How many copies will you need to make in a day?"

5. Analyze the price objection before answering it. What does the prospect mean, "The price is too high."? You need to know at least mentally, "Compared to what?" It may help to ask the simple question, "Do you mind telling me why you feel the price is too high?"

From the answer you can go to the matching answers why your price is fair by comparison.

6. Stress long-range values over small price differences. Say something like, "I understand your concern about price, but what you're most interested in is getting the most value for your money, isn't it?" Then recall the features that contribute extra value and their long-range benefits like more enjoyment, fewer repair costs, increased sales and profits.

7. Be ready to challenge price comparisons. Seldom are two products or services exactly alike. Even when they are physically similar, the fringe benefits that come with buying from one firm or the other come into the evaluation. When a prospect says, "I can get imprinted binders for less that that," you have to make sure that he or she is making fair comparisons. "Yes, I'm sure you're right. Binders come in all kinds of quality. But what you want, from what you've told me, is a quality binder that will impress your seminar registrants and will hold their materials safely for reference and referrals for years to come. Am I right?" Now resell the qualities that give those results.

If you are experienced in negotiations, you know that buyers will claim they can buy your product for less from a competitor when this may not be so. It is used as a tactic for getting the salesperson to panic and lower the price. You can't accuse the buyer of lying, but you can plant seeds of doubt that he or she will be getting something less at the lower price.

For example, "I'm surprised that City Merchandisers have quoted that price. Usually we are quite competitive. I wonder if it could be for last year's model or the one with the plastic trim. Let me go over again what you will be getting with this model which seems to suit your purposes most effectively . . ."

8. Minimize the price difference. When selling a higher quality item at a higher price, break the price difference between the higher and lower priced items into intervals spread over the life of the better quality item. "This mower will last longer than ten years, but let's just use a ten-year accounting life for comparison purposes. The extra $60 this better mower costs is just $6 a year or less than 50 cents a month. I'm sure you'll agree that being able to start the mower easier, get the mowing done sooner with the wider swath, and the other conveniences are well worth the 50 cents, don't you agree?"

9. Emphasize your added services. People are willing to pay more for an identical product when they are aware of desirable services that go with it but not with the lower priced one. Make a list of the advantages your customers get from buying from you and be ready to emphasize them when a price comparison comes up.

For example, "We remove all our computer components from their cartons and check them out carefully before we sell them to you. If anything goes wrong, we're always here to straighten it out quickly. If you need instruction, we have competent people on our staff to help you."

10. Make your higher price an asset. If your product or service is one that is consistently higher than competition but has the added value to back it up, you can use price as an asset rather than defending it as something undesirable.

Here are some examples. "Yes, are prices are a little higher than some others in our field. But we have consistently sold more year after year than those with cheaper merchandise. We couldn't do that if the values weren't good, could we?" "Yes, our price seems high for some shoppers. It frankly isn't made for the low-price market. It is geared for the customers who want high quality and are willing to pay the difference. But it gives you greater profit on every sale as a result." "Yes, I understand that brand is lower priced than ours. If we made it, we could probably sell it for the same price, too. But we prefer to go the higher quality route because we know that the customer pays less for quality in the long run."

7 Actions to Take When You Cannot Make Price Concessions

Sales negotiation infers that there will be concessions made by the buyer and seller. Yet many salespeople enter the negotiations with strict guidelines on price from which the salesperson cannot make concessions.

Here are some actions you can take that can substitute for your inability to give price concessions.

1. Emphasize your volume discount and package prices all customers get under the same conditions. "If you will order ten, I can reduce the price to just $16.39 each. Would that be okay?"

2. Assure the prospect that he is getting the lowest price anyone will get under the same conditions. As buyers, we are usually satisfied if we believe this. What upsets any buyer is to feel that someone else is getting a better deal. It's a matter of pride as well as economics.

3. If the prospect is comparison shopping, point out the fringe benefits of dealing with you and your firm. One salesperson tells his prospects, "When you buy from me, you get me with it." Your advice and ongoing suggestions add value to the basic cost of your products or service.

4. Repeat those features and benefits that seemed especially important during the presentation. Give them emphasis.

5. Point out the continued satisfactions promised. Back them up with testimonials and cases.

6. Make a guarantee within your power to do so. "I tell you what I'll do, Mr. Murphy. Let's start with just five cases and give them a thirty-day trial. If at the end of that time they haven't sold to your satisfaction, I'll take the rest back for full credit. Is it a deal?"

7. Make concession-like promises of things you will do in the future over which you have control. "I'll check your stock on hand on each call and make suggestions for re-order. I'll also make suggestions of what others are doing to increase their sales." See the following checklist for suggestions.

NON-PRICE CONCESSIONS CHECKLIST

Here are suggestions for additional benefits you can offer a prospect when you cannot reduce the price. Keep in mind that most of these will have a monetary value to you or your firm through time and expense involved. Treat their value just as you would comparable price dollars when offering them as concessions.

Prepare your own list of non-price concessions based on what you can do and are willing to do to get the order.

Standard quantity discount schedule	Extended warranty
Goods on consignment	Special warranties beyond standard one
Cancellation clause	Discount for immediate or early payment
Return privilege	Special payment terms
Service for a given period	Free storage agreement
Spare parts provided	Tests
Delivery concessions	Trial run
Assume delivery costs	Expert consultation and advice
Training of users	Engineering changes
Free training manuals	Territory protection where legal
Free literature	

7 Strategies for Making Price Concessions

Although professional salespeople will hold out as long as possible before making price concessions, they have to prepare for the time when such moves are necessary. Planning your strategies for the possibility of having to make price concessions is just as important as planning the rest of the sales call.

In Chapter 4 we discussed strategies for making any kind of concession during the sales negotiation. Let's review the main points brought out in that discussion to see how they would apply to making a price concession.

1. Start with your highest expectation in price. Above all, do NOT suggest to the buyer in any way during your presentation that you are willing to cut the price. Too many inexperienced salespeople feel compelled to open with something like, "By the way, keep in mind as I make our proposal that I'm prepared to give 25% discount on our published price." Where would the negotiations start?

2. Make price concessions in small amounts and do it thoughtfully, almost painfully. Use a scratch pad and calculator. Too large a concession, too easy, tells the buyer there's more available. Studies on negotiation show that losers give too much away on each concession.

3. Trade one concession for another. The best time to get a concession from the buyer is when you are offering one. "Let me see. (pause) I think I could cut the price about $37 if you could pick up the equipment at our warehouse. Could you do that?"

4. Make sure the buyer understands the full value of your concession. "Let me check to see if I can get a reduction of a half-cent a unit. That would mean a savings of about $485 on your total order. How does that sound?"

5. Understand all the other requirements before making the price concession. All the non-price concessions you may have already made will cost your firm money, too.

6. Before making the price concession, get a commitment to buy. "If I am able to get the price down 3%, are you ready to sign the order now?"

7. Be prepared to withdraw any price concession if the prospect doesn't buy. Concessions are just bargaining chips.

As brought out in Chapter 2, after buyers get you to cut a price, they may ask for another type of concession at the same price.

7 Tactics for Renewing the "Final Offer"

There comes a time in some sales negotiations when either the buyer of the salesperson says, "That's my final offer. Take it or leave it." The words may not be as blunt as this, but the meaning is the same. Unless somebody makes a concession or gets a better understanding of the sales proposal, the sales negotiation is over.

We covered this situation in Chapter 2 as a tactic the buyer may use to wring out further concessions from the salesperson. Review this discussion again. Here are the suggested tactics for renewing the "final offer" that were covered.

1. Continue with the negotiations as though you didn't hear the statement.

2. Assume that the buyer isn't really serious. Check it out with questions.

3. Review the terms of the proposal to see if you both agree on what they are.

4. Restate the benefits of accepting your proposal and the losses and risk in not accepting it.

5. Change the proposal package ingredients like lower quality or quantity, removing items, reducing services to reduce the price.

6. Isolate the problem factors and continue negotiations on the rest.

7. Give the buyer a chance to back away without losing face. Take the blame yourself for not making the benefits clear.

Negotiation Deadlock Means No Sale

We read about negotiations being deadlocked in treaties, trade discussions, congressional committees and labor-management negotiations. While nobody seems to like deadlocks, history shows that a party willing to bring negotiations to a deadlock more often settles eventually on better terms. Of course, the deliberate deadlock has also turned negotiators into losers, too.

Salespeople are quite familiar with the deadlock in sales negotiations. They call it "losing the sale." In spite of prior concessions by the buyer and the salesperson, the buyer doesn't agree to buy and the salesperson doesn't agree to any further concessions.

Salespeople certainly don't like deadlocks in a sales negotiation, but there comes a time when it may be necessary to say, "Well, I'm certainly sorry we couldn't come to an agreement for now, Miss Craig. If you don't mind, however, I'll check back with you in a couple of weeks and perhaps we can pick up where we left off."

The deadlock leaves both the prospect and the salesperson with a sense of failure that the sale didn't come off if the prospect is really interested in owning the product. They wonder if there was something each could have done differently, some concession that was overlooked. Should they have accepted the last offer? How will the deadlock affect their reputation up the management line?

Unfortunately, in today's business world, losing a sale is too often harder on the salesperson's reputation than making a sale that will be unprofitable. This encourages salespeople to agree to concessions in order to make a sale that will lose money for the firm.

Enlightened management, however, does not equate a deadlock or lost sale with failure. They know that it is often the case where the policies of the firm and the regulations under which the salespeople operate were the basic cause for the deadlock and the lost sale.

On rare occasions, the deadlock is used as a tactic to bring one party to a final concession. This is the "final offer" or "take-it-or-leave-it" tactic we discussed. This obviously involves risks, but may result in gains as well. When used by the salesperson, the profit is equal to the next concession.

But if the buyer says, "OK, no sale," the salesperson loses all the profit or commission. Unless the salesperson is certain that the prospect wants the product or service intensely, bringing the negotiation to a deadlock is a dangerous tactic.

Trade Price Concessions for Other Concessions

A major objective in all negotiations is not to trade off something of value without getting something else in return that is just as valuable or, hopefully, more valuable. In sales negotiation, experienced salespeople who are faced with having to make a price concession or some other concession of value, try to extract a concession of comparable value from the prospect. It's just part of the win-win objective for the sale where both the buyer and the salesperson are satisfied with the final terms.

Strangely enough, studies have shown that buyers are happier with purchases where they have had to make reasonable concessions than with a purchase where the price they offered was accepted too easily. They worried that they might have got an even better price had they asked for it.

Part of your planning for the sales negotiation should be a determination of "trading chips" you are prepared to ask for in return for any price concessions you may be required to make to close the sale.

The advanced planning is important because it prepares you to ask for something specific in return for a price concession. But part of your planning should also be to determine ahead of time the value of the concession to you or your firm compared to the price reduction you will make. You obviously want the values to be relatively the same. Here are some suggestions of areas in which you can ask for trade-offs from the buyer in return for a lower price. They can also be used when you are asked to make a non-price concession like training the employees or extending the service warranty. "Yes, if you buy the equipment we recommend in the proposal, we will take five of your staff through our training workshop without charge."

YOUR TRADE-OFF CHECKLIST

1. Increased volume. Ask the buyer to increase the quantity of the purchase. "I can reduce the price one cent a pound if you will increase your order to a million pounds. Will you do that?"

2. Change in specifications. Ask the buyer permission to omit something in the specifications that add to the cost of the product. "If you are willing to have the cover in two colors instead of four, we can reduce the price of the printing $325."

3. Add other items. Ask the buyer to increase the total sale by adding other items to the list. "If you agree to take the service contract on the machine for two years, I can reduce the price five percent."

4. Longer contract period. Extending the contract reduces your cost of sales. "If we can have your floor maintenance contract for two years instead of one, I can give you an extra month of service free."

5. Less costly packaging. If the buyer does not require your highest cost packaging, offer a saving on less expensive packaging. "Since you use this item in large quantities in your own plant, there is no need to put them in individual packages. If we can put them in cartons of twenty five units, we can reduce the price five cents a unit."

6. Buyer absorbs shipping costs. Shipping costs can be a considerable expense for some products. Some customers may prefer to pick up the merchandise and pay less. "If you can have the furniture picked up at our warehouse, I can reduce the price by $75."

7. Buyer unpacks and sets up merchandise. Some products like furniture and machines are often delivered, unpacked, checked and installed by the seller. If the buyer will take over this job, the savings can be used to reduce the price. "If we can deliver these in their original cartons and you unpack and set them up, we can take five percent off the price."

8. Early payment. Cash flow is important to any firm and money that comes in ahead of the anticipated date is money that doesn't have to be borrowed. Collection expense is also avoided by cash or assured payments.

So discounts for cash or early payment are usually offered by the sellers. "We can offer you a 2% discount if you pay within ten days of receiving the merchandise." Check with your financial group on what they're willing to give up in price for cash and early payments.

Time to Close the Sale

When the buyer's objections and resistance have been handled satisfactorily, it's time to close the sales negotiations.

We'll cover the techniques and strategies successful salespeople use to reach this final goal in Chapter 10.

10
Closing the Sales Negotiation

No Close, No Sale!

THERE is no better means for identifying professional salespeople than through their ability to close the sales negotiation with an order. When two or more salespeople are compared, the final rankings are inevitably based on sales volume, their relative ability to get the orders.

Finding prospects, making calls, performing well during a presentation, and all the other techniques of selling are obviously important elements in gaining a higher percentage of sales. But the final test is whether or not the salesperson can end the negotiation with a sale. Unless the prospect agrees to buy, now or at a definite later date, the sales negotiation effort has been wasted.

A successful industrial salesman once made this simple statement to a group of new salespeople, "Your sale is not completed until you get a signed purchase order or ring the cash register."

Pleasant relations with a prospect are obviously important, but it takes an order to make a customer and to pay the salary or commission.

All Negotiators Want to Close

Negotiations on any matter are brought to a close when each party feels that all the concessions are made that will be made and that further negotiation attempts will not be worth while. One or the other party initiates the closing action and the agreement is drawn up and signed.

In sales negotiations, the salesperson is the party that normally brings about the closing action. Sales trainers over the years have developed many techniques for this important step . . . closing the sale.

Sometimes the prospect or customer will surprise the salesperson by saying, "OK, I'll take it" during the presentation. Don't expect this to happen often, however. Always be ready with a strategy to lead the prospect or customer into making a buying decision before you consider the sales negotiation closed.

The decision the salesperson seeks at the end of a particular sales negotiation might not be to buy a product or service. It may be an agreement with the prospect that is just one step in an eventual sale several negotiation sessions down the line. It might be permission to make a survey, for example, or an agreement by the prospect to visit installations made for other customers.

Whatever the immediate objective for a sales negotiation call, the techniques for reaching it are basically the same as for getting a normal buying decision.

Help the Prospect Make Decisions Leading to the Sale

People need help in making the buying decision. Reluctance to buy is perfectly normal. The professional salesperson knows this, and takes the initiative to bring the sale to a close after a favorable decision by the prospect.

High pressure selling is out of place today. But there is nothing wrong with leading the prospect into making a buying decision by means of well-defined closing techniques. High pressure selling aims at getting the order regardless of the prospect's needs or desires.

Professional negotiation closing techniques are aimed at moving prospects into making buying decisions after they are convinced that the product or service is the best solution to their needs and desires.

Closing is the Last Step in Sales Negotiations

Closing the sale is the logical last step in sales negotiation. All the other efforts in a sales call are preparation for the closing step, so don't stop short of the objective.

The sales call is like having the order sealed up inside a room that is protected by a tumbler lock. The salesperson inserts the key to the lock when he or she opens the sale. One by one the tumblers inside the lock line up as the salesperson makes the presentation and handles objections. When they all line up, the salesperson turns the key with closing persuasiveness and opens the door to the order.

Don't be Afraid to Close!

Why do some salespeople fail to close? Lots of studies have been made on this important problem, and the most logical answer to emerge is FEAR. Nobody likes to feel rejected, to be turned down. As long as the salesperson keeps talking, there's no risk of being turned down. But when we ask for the order, we face the chance of being rejected, so there is the urge to put it off a little longer. The salesperson may also fear that once the prospect refuses to buy, the whole session is over and the sale is lost.

Keep talking, he reasons, and the chances are better that the prospect will be convinced to buy. Unfortunately, talking too long is more apt to lose the sale than to save it.

If you were to ask professional salespeople for their one great rule for closing, they would probably say, "Don't wait too long." Too many salespeople talk themselves out of a sale by prolonging it until the prospect thinks up more good reasons for not buying or becomes tired and wants to put off the decision.

The early attempt to close may not work, but if it does, think of the time you save for other sales or for rounding up more prospects!

When Is the Best Time To Close?

There is no magic time to try to close the sale. We hear now and then that someone has discovered one and is willing to sell his secret to other salespeople.

But it turns out that there is no universal signal or body language the prospect uses to tell the salesperson, "I'm ready to buy now if you'll just ask me for the order."

Professional salespeople do consciously observe the prospect's reactions to the sales presentation, however. When the reactions to specific features, benefits or proofs are favorable, the salesperson tries for a close.

This is called the "trial close" by professionals and we will discuss its use later.

Learn to Interpret the Buyer's Body Language

Salespeople are coached to interpret the prospect's body language as the sale progresses to try to identify the right climate for asking for the order.

At first, the prospect may sit back, expressionless or frowning, arms folded, legs crossed, perhaps fumbling with papers on the desk while the salesperson talks. Then he begins to relax his position, unfolds his arms, leans forward when certain benefits are mentioned, smiles and his eyes widen. Now he examines the samples, reads the literature and testimonial letters, asks questions. These are all physical signals of growing interest in buying that should tell the salesperson to try for a close soon.

More coming on Body Language

We will discuss Body Language more fully in Chapter 12 as part of developing your listening skills. You have to "listen" to the buyer's body language as well as what he or she is saying verbally.

Questions and Objections Are Buying Signals

The prospect's questions are the most significant buying signals. Asking the price is a sign of interest in buying even when the prospect says the price is too high. He wouldn't be interested in ANY price if he wasn't interested in owning the product or service. Questions like, "When can I get delivery," or "When would I have to pay for it?" mean that the prospect has mentally signed the order except for details. Questions on the guarantee, selections available, terms of sale, minimum quantities, service, training of employees, all are signals to the salesperson to stop selling and start the closing action.

Don't insist on making your complete presentation when these signals occur. Stop when the prospect appears to be convinced and make a trial close. Keep on talking and you may lose the sale.

Even an objection can be a buying signal. This is particularly true when prospects show that they would like to own the product or service, but something is keeping them from buying. Uncover the objection, answer it satisfactorily or negotiate a compromise and the sale can be closed.

Start With Easy Agreements

In any negotiations where the parties may be somewhat suspicious of each other, the agenda is usually to get agreements on relatively minor issues first. As these are resolved satisfactorily, trust is built gradually and the parties feel better about discussing the more difficult issues.

While this is going on, each party has a chance to test the reactions of the other without too much risk.

In sales negotiations, the salesperson and the buyer follow much the same procedure except that it is not quite as serious as in international negotiations.

The major problem is whether the prospect will agree to the salesperson's proposal, usually a buying decision.

Both the salesperson and the prospect usually prefer to start with minor agreements, even on matters like the weather.

Each feature and benefit the salesperson presents, each question and answer, constitute step by step agreements that finally culminate in the most important one . . . will the prospect buy?

As you will see in our discussion of ways to close the sale, even the decision to buy can be arrived at by minor decisions like when delivery is most convenient, how the customer prefers to pay for the merchandise, or whether she prefers the red or the blue jacket.

Use Questions To Get Commitments

Instead of answering questions directly, use them to get commitments to buy if possible.

For example, suppose a prospect flashes a buying signal question like, "How soon could I get a machine like this one?" Most salespeople would answer it directly, like "Oh, in about a week." The prospect would probably nod, keep quiet, and the salesperson would keep on selling. But suppose you replied with another question, "How soon do you need it?" If the prospect answers, "I'd like it in about a week," you can begin writing up the order because the prospect has committed himself to buy if delivery can be made in a week.

Questions can be used during the sales presentation to get small commitments which can be added together later to get the big decision, the one to buy.

For example, a salesperson might say, "This frame is made of stainless steel which will last you longer because it won't rust out." That's a good point, but the prospect may not think of it as a reason to buy. The salesperson can add the question, "Wouldn't you prefer an aquarium that doesn't have to be replaced in a few years?" to encourage the prospect to make a favorable decision.

After a few more demonstrations of features and benefits, the salesperson reviews the commitments with the prospect and tries for the close, perhaps on a minor issue. "You have agreed that you prefer the stainless steel frame and the larger thirty gallon tank. I can deliver this model on our Thursday delivery or would you prefer to take it with you so you can start enjoying it right away?"

6 BASIC WAYS TO CLOSE THE SALE

We could easily describe a hundred specific techniques successful salespeople use to close sales. There are whole books devoted to just closing the sale. But if we were to study all these techniques and tactics, we would find that they would all fit into six basic ways to close the sale. As we discuss them, plan how you would use the principle to fit into your own strategy for closing your sales.

1. The Trial Close. The first attempt to close the sale is usually considered a Trial Close. It is usually more of a check on how the prospect is reacting to the proposition, but if it results in an actual sale, a lot of valuable time can be saved.

The Trial Close is usually in the form of a question along the lines of the Assumptive Close, like "How many gallons do you think you would use in a month?" The question gets the prospect's reaction without forcing him to make a clear yes or no decision on buying.

If the salesperson forces the prospect to say no to buying too early, it is difficult to get him to change his mind. For example, "Let me put you down for three gross."

The questions used in a Trial Close are designed to get reactions rather than commitments, but their answers tell the salesperson if the time is right to go for the final close. If it isn't, objections will probably come out so the salesperson can answer them and try another trial close.

You might think of your questions as including the unspoken words, "If you bought this . . ." Here are examples where this would be implied: "Which size would be most appropriate for you?" "Which colors would go better with your walls?" "Where would you install this machine?" Don't get discouraged if the Trial Close doesn't work the first time. It seldom does. But don't give up too soon. Handle resistance, then try another close until you observe final buying signals or are convinced the prospect can't be sold.

2. The Assumptive Close. This is the prime closing technique. All of the other strategies for closing are actually related to it. The professional salesperson comes into every sales negotiation with the assumption that the prospect will buy the product or service. When the salesperson has presented the proposal to the point that the prospect understands it, needs it and wants it, the salesperson starts to close by assuming that the prospect will buy.

Then the close is merely the working out of details of getting the right product or service into the possession of the buyer.

The Assumptive Close is usually a question on a point which, if answered affirmatively, implies that the prospect will buy. A key word in this type of close is "When?" For example, the salesperson asks, "When would you want your refrigerator delivered?" If the prospect wants your product, there is a time when he wants it. By centering his attention on the question of time, you require him to decide to buy without his being aware of any forcing.

Assume the prospect WILL buy, and close on the minor details.

Fear keeps the average salesperson from using this highly successful closing strategy. Fear that the customer will say, "Hold it! I didn't say I was going to buy it." But what if he does? Just treat it as a trial close and find out why he doesn't want to buy yet. You need to know that, too, so what can you lose? But if he doesn't object, the sale is closed.

The Assumptive Close works best when the prospect finds it easier to go along with the salesperson than to turn him down. The salesperson asks, "How soon would you have to have this?" It is easier for the prospect to specify a time than to put up more sales resistance . . . provided that he has already determined that he would like to own the product.

3. The Alternative or "Which One" Close. "Give the prospect a choice," is a great rule of selling. The choice, however, should always be between something and something, either of which results in a sale, never between something or nothing.

The Alternative or "Which One" Close uses this technique to get the prospect to make a decision that leads to the sale. You can see that this is an expansion of both the Assumptive and the Trial Closes.

It is used when you are more certain that the prospect is receptive to your product or service. It is closer to the signing of the order. In fact, it may follow a Trial Close that turned out right and becomes the actual clincher to the sale.

The word, "Which" is the key to this close. Common choices in this closing technique are, which color; which size; which model; which finish; which method of payment or delivery? It is always a choice between two or more alternatives. The information you require on your order blank will suggest questions to ask, like how many, model number, sizes, quantities, where shipped?

There are other ways of wording the key question, of course. Here are some examples of giving the prospect a choice, either of which would lead to closing the sale:

"Would you like this portable model or would you prefer the console?"

"When would you prefer to make the payments, at the first of the month or toward the end?"

"Do you want this in your name or your wife's name?"

"Do you want your policy sent to your office or home?"

"Would you want all one color or do you want me to mix them?"

4. The Action Close. The Action Close is frequently expressed as simply, "Ask for the order." Many otherwise lost sales could be saved if the salesperson would simply say, "Well, that's the story, Mr. James. Shall we go ahead on that basis?"

You make up the prospect's mind for him and get his verification.

The Action Close should not be attempted until the prospect shows signs of being receptive. It may follow a Trial Close that gets a positive reaction from the prospect. The action is a tool for making up the prospect's mind to act.

Professional closers may DO something as well as SAY something to bring about the close. At the right time, they introduce a proposal to action that will close the sale automatically unless the prospect stops them. For example, the salesperson might say, "You seem to prefer the 127 model machine. Let me call our warehouse to see if we have one in stock." If the prospect lets the salesperson call, the sale can be assumed closed except for details of payment and delivery.

This close is an extension of the Assumptive Close because you start an action that assumes a close unless the prospect stops you.

Perhaps the most common action close consists of writing up the order, then showing it to the prospect and asking a question like, "Would you verify this description? I'll arrange to deliver it on whatever day you specify." Avoid words like "sign here," or "sign this order." People tend to shun legal-sounding actions.

If the development of the sales presentation involves a survey of the prospect's needs, the salesperson can use the results of the survey in an action close.

For example, he might say, "Here is what we found you need, Mr. Foster. If you will verify the list, we can start saving you money on your operation by next Wednesday. Or would you want to get started sooner?"

If the list has been written on an order form or contract, his verification can be his signature to the order.

5. The Summary Close. The Summary Close is frequently combined with the Action Close. Some sales involve several individual items or services. These can be listed by the salesperson on a piece of paper or an order blank. In leading to the close, the salesperson might say, "Now let me go over what you will get with this installation." After she reads the list, she says, "Can you think of anything we missed?"

If the prospect says no, the sale is closed. If he names some items not on the list, the sales is closed after the items are added. The decision to buy was already accomplished and the close became a matter of negotiation the details.

The Summary Close can be used for a review of the features and benefits which appeared to make the greatest impression on the prospect. "You seemed to prefer the larger rooms, the recreation room, the more modern kitchen and the closeness to schools which the Baldwin house has. Shall we submit them an offer, say, of $153,000?"

Be ready for the prospect's statement that he wants to think it over. This is a favorite method for avoiding making the decision to buy. Ask, "What do you need to think over that I might have missed?" Or you might say, "That's what you should do. Let's think it over together. Which point do you want clarified?"

Another way is to start the decision-making process now, like, "Which features did you like best?" "Is there anything you object to?"

After the prospect expresses his opinions, the salesperson knows which benefits to emphasize and what questions remain unanswered. After these are covered, the salesperson tries for another close.

6. The Inducement Close. Every prospect has a tendency to want to postpone the decision to buy. Salespeople want the prospect to buy now because they know that their chances of making the sale become less and less as time goes by.

The incentives the salesperson uses to persuade the prospect to buy now instead of later can be included under the heading of the Inducement Close. Some of these inducements could be a type of concession in some cases as mentioned in Chapter 9.

Some inducements are pre-arranged by the firm as a premium in the promotion of the product or service, like free service for a year, a case of detergent with a washing machine, or a discount in price for a limited time.

The Inducement Close is good only if the prospect is sold on the satisfaction of his need and only requires a little shove to buy now instead of later.

Fear of loss can be as strong an inducement to buy now as hope of gain. Many business people who might not be interested in making a little more profit will fight hard to keep from losing what they have now.

So the salesperson might remind the prospect, "Each day you operate without this improved system costs you money. Let's make the changes immediately so you can start cutting your labor costs as soon as possible."

Here are some other examples of how you can induce prospects to buy now.

"When the next shipment comes in, we'll have to charge the increased price."

"We have just one table in stock with that finish. It will take about six weeks to get another one for you."

"The sale ends tomorrow. After that you'll have to pay an additional $27."

You will find additional examples in Chapter 4 as part of the non-price concessions.

If You Can't Get the Concession, Take a Promise

Sales negotiations depend upon concessions to arrive at the terms of the sale, the final agreement. When the buyer can't or won't make the concessions you would like, be receptive to taking a promise for something of value in the future in order to close the present sale. The buyer might say, for example, "If you will let us have them for that price, I will personally see to it that you will get all of our so-and-so business for next year."

Sure, promises are not as enforceable as contracts, but they do have value when made by honorable buyers and sellers who take pride in keeping their word. They're the next best thing to a concession.

Salespeople can also make a promise that could swing the sale when a price concession isn't possible. For example, "I have to hold to that price, but I can promise that you'll have the merchandise whenever you need it even if I have to bring it to you in person."

Use the Salami Strategy

Members of the Communist Party were well known for using what was called the "salami strategy" to carve away small concessions from the other parties in international negotiations. The idea is that if you can get thin slices often enough, you will end up with the "whole salami." Asking for the whole salami at the beginning usually fails, but tiny pieces sliced off are hardly noticed and when they are, the amount is so small that it is accepted.

If you are negotiating to get the prospect to switch from a competitor to you, and there is reluctance on the part of the prospect due to a mixture of current satisfaction and a degree of loyalty, ask for a slice of the business as an alternative. "Let's try this, Mr. James. Let me have the order for just half of the chemicals you need for the next quarter. Then you compare our quality and service with that of your present supplier."

If that doesn't work, try a thinner slice. "You may be right. Perhaps providing just a third of the amount would give us both a fair test. Do you think that three months is long enough or would six months be a better test?"

The prospect doesn't risk much by making the minor decision to give you a piece of the business compared to making the larger decision of giving it all to you. Obviously you must do everything you can to make the trial run a success so you can come back to negotiations for all of the business, or once again, another slice of it.

Develop Your Own Closing Techniques

In this Chapter we covered the six basic strategies successful salespeople use to close sales. Become so familiar with them that you can combine two or more when needed to close a sales negotiation more effectively. Develop your own techniques for using these strategies in your own particular selling situations.

Books on selling in general and on Closing in particular, will give examples you may want to try out for yourself.

Observe other salespeople both in and out of your product or service field. When you observe a closing tactic being used, consider how you might use it in your own selling situation.

Your product or service, your own personality and your experience with closing tactics will dictate the techniques that will work best for you.

An important addition to your closing strategies should be to compliment the buyer on his or her decisions. You want to leave the customers feeling that the sale was a good one and that they want to buy from you again.

Turndowns Come With the Territory

Professional salespeople use various closing techniques, but there is a common thread running through all their strategies. The professionals aren't afraid to ask for the order!

They don't consider a turndown as a personal insult or rejection. They try to close early and then try again if that fails. If they can't persuade the prospect to buy now, they try to settle for a sale at a future date.

And even if all attempts to close fail, they keep the door open for further contacts as long as the buyer is a qualified prospect worth the continuing effort.

Know When To Concede

There comes a time in any sales negotiation when both the buyer and the salesperson must know when to stop the demands and when to concede. A critical point in any type of negotiation is when one of the parties says, "That's enough. I quit!" If this point is reached, the party that quits often refuses to negotiate further even when the second party backs down. When this happens, both parties lose. This situation in sales negotiations was covered in Chapter 9 along with suggestions for getting the negotiation with the prospect started again. But you have to acquire a practical sense of when to concede another point in order to make a decent sale and when to refuse so as not to wind up with an unprofitable order.

Since the ideal sales negotiation philosophy has both parties coming out with needs satisfied, both professional buyers and professional salespeople try to agree on terms that are favorable but still short of demanding the last possible concession.

Make This Book Your Sales Negotiation Handbook

This is the end of Part II and our integration of the strategies and tactics of negotiation with those of professional selling from opening to closing the sales negotiation.

Part III and the final two Chapters provide additional suggestions on the practical use of two important tools of selling and negotiation, asking questions and listening.

By now, you probably feel like most professional salespeople that there is too much to learn about sales negotiation in such a short time. And you're right.

Don't expect to be able to remember and use all of the suggestions offered here. Use the book now as a valuable reference when planning future sales negotiations and evaluating those you feel should have gone better.

Some of the world's great government and business negotiators confess that they learn new strategies and tactics constantly as they watch their opponents perform. They aren't afraid to change old ways and try new ones. But while they continue to learn by experience, they retain and reuse those strategies that worked before in similar circumstances.

Keep Improving Your Negotiative Selling Skills

While the purpose of this book was to bring together those negotiation strategies and tactics that work best for salespeople, there was no way we could cover that vast field known as negotiation. You will have to continue learning all you can about negotiations because your skills will be valuable not only in your selling career but also in any contacts you have with people, in your own purchases and in negotiating your personal affairs.

Keep reading the good books on negotiation in general as they come out. Watch other salespeople as they use negotiation tactics on other people as well as yourself. Attend workshops on negotiation when they are conducted in your area or by your company.

Make changes in your worksheets or write notes to yourself on ideas you get for better questions to ask or actions to take that can give you the edge during the sales negotiations. Keep a good mental inventory of your existing negotiation powers so you are ready to use them whenever the sales situation warrants.

Keep building these powers to give you the advantages you should have when calling on prospects and customers and dealing with your competition.

The Professional Sales Negotiator

Being a good sales negotiator takes time and effort. But it pays off in increased sales. More than that, it gives you the recognition and personal gratification that only expertise and true professionalism can offer.

PART III:

Increasing Your Questioning and Listening Skills

11

How to Use Questions in Sales Negotiation

It Takes Questions to Get Answers

PERSUASIVE sales negotiation depends on the effective use of questions by the salesperson to get the prospects to express their needs, desires and prejudices. Once these are uncovered by skillful questioning, the right decisions become obvious for both the salesperson and the prospect.

Sales negotiators use questions to get feedback on what the prospect or customer is thinking. This feedback serves two primary purposes . . . to check the progress of communication and to uncover clues as to the real needs and wants of the customer.

Based on the information obtained through questioning, the salesperson corrects misunderstandings and alters the presentation to put more stress on those features and benefits of the product or service that the clues suggest would best match the needs and desires of the prospect.

The feedback obtained through questions is particularly helpful in uncovering the real causes of resistance to buying so they can be answered satisfactorily.

More questions, less talk

The inexperienced salesperson talks and shows, then talks some more until the prospect withdraws, loses interest or even becomes antagonistic. Through planned questions, however, the salesperson draws the prospects out and leads them into making the decisions and concessions the salesperson is after in the negotiation.

When a prospect is guided through questions into making a decision himself, he is more convinced of its correctness and will defend it vigorously. The same proposal he might have challenged or refused if made by the salesperson becomes his own decision to uphold.

The author's book, *The Salesman's Guide to More Effective Selling,* was the first selling guide to devote separate chapters to selling through questions and listening. During the research on effective questioning for the book, the author studied the techniques used by labor and international negotiators to question parties in negotiations and by lawyers in questioning witnesses.

When the idea of combining negotiation skills with selling skills was conceived, it became apparent that the same questioning skills the salesperson had learned and practiced for persuading prospects to buy would work even more effectively when the salesperson added negotiating skills to selling.

Kipling Had Six Words for Salespeople

When Rudyard Kipling wrote these lines back in 1902, he could have had salespeople in mind.

> *I keep six honest serving-men*
> *(They taught me all I knew)*
> *Their names are What and Why and When*
> *And How and Where and Who*

These same six words are the key words professional salespeople use to get the information they need for persuading prospects to see things their way during the negotiations. Here are examples of how they are used. Keep them in mind and practice using each of these "serving men" to help you close more sales.

"WHAT is the main problem you have in . . . ?"
"WHY do you think the work piles up at that point?"
"WHEN would be the best time to . . .?"
"HOW could this plan be altered to . . .?"
"WHERE do you think this would work best?"
"WHO else would be involved in making the decision?"

3 Basic Types of Questions for Negotiation

There are a number of ways in which questions can be classified depending upon their purpose and use. Questions for probing for information and for getting agreement as in sales negotiation, however, are usually considered in three basic forms.

1. Open or Non-Directive Questions. These are questions structured so the prospect or customer cannot answer with a yes or no. They require the person to give an opinion or relate an experience. For example:

"What do you think of . . .?"
"What has been your experience with . . .?"
"How do you feel about . . .?"

The open or non-directive question is designed to draw the prospect out, to get answers that will tell the salesperson what the true needs and desires are so he or she can stress the features and benefits that best match them. This type of question will also bring out reasons for buying resistance so the salesperson can handle them.

Open questions make the prospects more comfortable and secure than the closed type that require a yes or no answer. Since open questions require some thought rather than a quick yes or no response, the prospect tends to give more consideration to the salesperson's proposition.

Since open questions usually ask for an opinion, they show the prospects that their opinions are valued by the salesperson and this encourages better communication.

2. Directive or Structured Questions. Directed, or closed, questions require the prospect to give a specific answer, like a definite amount of money, an actual date or time. They require expansion or further explanation on a particular point and help maintain two-way communication.

Usually, the directive question is used in conjunction with open or reflective questions to get more specific information. For example, "That was an interesting experience. When did that happen?"

The directive question is a little more threatening to the prospect than an open question because it calls for specific information which he or she might be unwilling to divulge. Weaving them into the interview with open and reflective questions gives a better understanding of the prospect's point of view and makes them less threatening to the prospect.

Here are examples of directive questions:

"How long do you think it would take to make the move?"
"How much would the savings be in a year?"
"What would be the best way to handle the repairs?"
"Did you know they were going into receivership?"

When used properly, directive questions can encourage the prospects to concentrate on areas of agreement rather than disagreement and allow the prospects the opportunity to convince themselves.

3. Reflective Questions. As the name implies, a reflective question repeats or rephrases in the saleperson's words what the prospect says or seems to infer. Reflective questions are usually a response to the prospect's answer to an open or nondirective question. Their usual purpose is to clarify understanding of what the prospect really means or feels.

But they can also be used to play back what the prospect said in the hope that he will modify his stand, to back off a little. The use of reflective questions calls for careful listening, selectivity and great care that the question does not reflect on the prospect's intelligence.

The reflective question helps avoid arguments because by using it the salesperson does not accept or reject the prospect's statements. It results in clarifying understanding between the prospect and the salesperson.

If the reflected question is not correct, the prospect will correct the thought. For example, the salesperson says, "You feel that this product would work for you if it could be made of copper instead of vinyl." The prospect may not have said it that way but merely expressed a preference for copper. If the prospect agrees to the statement, the salesperson can assume that the sale is made if the change to copper is possible.

As the example shows, a reflective question is more often spoken as a statement without the rising inflection of a question mark. Raising the voice or adding "is that so?" to the end would make it a true question, but the reflective statement works as well or better. Stating it as a question carries with it the feeling that you can't believe what the prospect is saying, that he must be a little strange.

Here is another example of the reflected question in statement form. The customer says, "That might work for your other customers, but our business is different." The salesperson responds with, "Your situation is completely different."

The reflected statement gets the same reaction as a question because it requires the prospect to agree or disagree with it. In this case, the prospect did not say "completely", and the salesperson hopes that the prospect will back off a bit to "a little different". The salesperson can then probe to see what the true differences are to show that the product or service can handle the difference or be modified to do so.

Reflective questions, particularly in statement form, create a better climate for agreement by sharing the prospect's feelings. Often when the salesperson shows that he or she understands the prospect's view, the prospect may drop a bad idea or correct an opinion after hearing it repeated by the salesperson.

For example, an exchange may go like this, starting with the salesperson's reflective question. "You would NEVER use carpeting in the reception area." "No, we never have, but I know that many firms do." "Yes, many do. They find that in addition to the added attractiveness for clients, and less noise, keeping the area clean is actually easier." "You have to be kidding. How is that possible?" Now the salesperson has an opening for persuading the prospect to switch to carpeting for the reception area.

A reflective question or statement also shows that the salesperson was listening, a reinforcement, and the prospect is encouraged to continue talking.

Key words for the reflective question technique are: You feel; you believe; what you're saying is . . .

Questions for Opening the Sales Negotiation

Professional salespeople use questions throughout the sales negotiation to get the prospect's reactions and to check the progress of communications. Even before sales trainers were exploring better ways to use questions in selling, salespeople were using them successfully to handle objections and close sales.

But one of the most important uses for questions that has gained the professional salespeople's interest in recent years is during in the opening of the sale, the first few minutes with the prospect.

In opening the sales negotiation, you must get the prospect's attention and interest quickly and the question is a great device for doing that. To answer your question, the prospects must break their attention from what they were thinking or doing when you appeared. They have to focus their attention on you to give you an answer.

The questions used in opening the sales negotiation are usually developed around the use of the product or service you are selling or the prospect's need that could be solved with them.

People respond affirmatively to any reasonable question put to them in the proper manner. We all do this out of habit and common courtesy. If the question involves a challenge, our interest is quickly aroused.

Some salespeople prefer to first ask permission to ask a few questions rather than starting right in with them. This alerts the prospect to the coming questions and massages their ego by acknowledging their importance. The request might take these forms:

"Mr. Walker, do you mind if I ask you a few questions about your printing requirements?"

"Mr. Ferguson, I have an idea that might save you time and money on your payroll processing but I want to be sure. May I ask you a few questions?"

The questions asked during the opening moments must be designed to get the kind of answers that will help the salesperson to proceed more intelligently with the sales presentation. Make-talk questions, like "How's business?" are not only useless, they could invite trouble. If the prospect says business is bad, you win only if you have a suggestion for improving it.

Here are some examples that will help you form your own questions. Your goal is to ask for information that will help you tailor your presentation to the customer's needs and wants.

"What brands of . . . are you selling now?"

"How long have you had them?"

"What is your biggest problem in (selling or using your product or service category)?"

"When do you consider changing brands or adding new ones?"

"Who makes the decision for adding new lines?"

"Where do you go if you need . . .?"

Tantalizer Questions for Openers

Here are some opening and lead-in questions which stimulate the prospect's attention and interest. Use them as examples for similar questions to fit your own sales presentations.

"How would you like to have . . . ?"

"Did you know that . . . ?"

"If I could show you . . . would you be interested?"

"Can you imagine . . .?"

"Suppose that . . . what would be your reaction?"

"Have you ever seen . . .?"

"Have you heard about (another customer)'s installation?"

Use Probing Questions

Use questions to probe for facts and feelings that help you tailor your presentation to the prospect's needs. Questions can also be used during the opening moments to qualify the prospects, to determine if they are worth more time. Strictly fact-finding questions can be asked of other employees during the pre-approach or qualifying period. The more pertinent questions should be saved for the person who can authorize the purchase.

The probing begins with questions whose answers will qualify the need for your products or service and the problems that could open the door to a sale. Here are some examples:

"How many office workers do you have?"

"Do you have your own floor maintenance crew?

One of the goals for probing questions is to get the prospect to express a problem the salesperson could solve with his or her products or service. Without a problem, there can be no sale.

The salesperson's solutions through the products or service must be matched with the prospect's problems that the questions expose.

Ask Questions That Get the Prospect's Opinion

One line of questioning used successfully by professional salespeople involves getting the prospect's opinion of situations involving other people or firms. Here is an example. "A recent article in the Wall Street Journal said that more business firms are saving on floor maintenance costs by carpeting the offices. How do you feel about that?" Whatever the prospect's reply, the floor covering salesperson now has a good opening for the presentation.

Other questions to get the prospect's opinion can be structured around what other customers have said, news items, government reports, any third party situation. After giving the statement, the salesperson asks questions like,

"Does this happen to you often?"
"Have you ever been concerned about this?"

After several probing questions have brought out the prospect's needs, problems and desires, you can use the responses to make a proposal. You might say, for example, "Based on what you have told me, I suggest we . . ." Sometimes you can bring in a story of how another customer solved a similar problem with your product or service. It's difficult to refuse to listen to how another person resolved a problem we're having.

Questions to Keep the Prospect Talking

It usually takes more than a few answers to your early questions to get to the root of the problems. You have to keep the prospect talking so more details and opinions come out. The techniques for keeping the prospect talking are classified by the psychologists as reinforcement. Reinforcement is a form of reward for doing something. We tend to keep doing something when we are rewarded for doing it. We tend to stop doing it when we are ignored or punished. You can reward your prospects and keep them talking by:

Praise for the action the prospect took.
Showing approval for the right answers, ignoring the wrong ones.
Repeating the prospect's statement or key words.

The reward through approval need not be a production number. A nod of the head, a smile, a single word like "Excellent!" or just an approving sound like "uh-huh" and an expectant look can keep the prospect talking.

When prospects seem to be slowing down or cutting off the explanations, you can use questions which are designed to keep them bringing out more information. Some examples would be:

"Then what happened?"
"How did it turn out?"
"What do you think caused it?"
"Are there any other reasons why you feel that way?"
"Suppose the colors had faded, what would have happened?"

Questions to Check the Prospect's Reaction

Every so often in a sales presentation, you should find out how the prospect is reacting to your proposition, whether or not you are really communicating. Is the prospect enthused or getting bored? Does the prospect understand your language? Does the prospect accept what you are saying?

The right questions will help you to determine the progress of the interview so you can back up or re-route the presentation to a final acceptance.

You obviously can't be as direct with your questions as you might want to be, like, "Say, am I boring you?" or "Do you understand what I'm talking about?" The questions should be worded to get a response that requires some thought if possible. But even questions that require just a simple yes or no or a nod of the head can be helpful in checking the progress of your interview and keeping the prospect's attention.

Here are some examples:

"How does that sound to you?"
"How would this work in your situation?"
"Would you like to have the same results?"
"Could this apply to your system?"
"Has this ever happened to you?"
"Do you agree with his remarks?"

Insert questions like these into your sales presentation at convenient spots.

Questions to Probe Deeper

To get to the prospect's true motives or the real objection, you have to get a more telltale reaction than simple answers to your questions. The questions designed to keep the prospect talking will bring more information out, but there are times when we want to do more than to reward or reinforce. We may even want to antagonize to get more information on which to build the sales negotiation.

Here are typical questions for getting the prospects to tell you more after they have made a statement or stopped talking.

"Why do you say that?" (Or just, "Why?")
"In what way?"
"Would you say the same thing if . . .?"
"Suppose we could . . ."

Repeat a key word or phrase as a question and WAIT for more amplification. Examples:

"The colors faded?"
"What do you have in mind?"
"What do you think causes that?"
"Do you have any other reasons for feeling as you do?"

Questions to Assure Understanding

It is sometimes difficult to determine if prospects really understand your presentation or proposal. Yet they have to understand it the way you intended before taking the action you want.

Just asking, "Do you understand?" isn't enough. Saying yes doesn't mean that the prospect understands. He may think he understands without really doing so. He may not understand but doesn't want to admit it. Buying your proposal may not be important enough at that stage to risk the embarassment of showing ignorance.

A better way to check understanding is to ask questions and let the answers tell you if you have communicated effectively. For example, after mentioning a feature and benefit, ask, "Would this be an improvement over the equipment you're using now?" or, "How does that compare with your present machine?"

Communication has to be two-way, so you have to be sure you understand the prospect's statements correctly before you alter your presentation. Here you can use questions for clarification, usually associated with a restatement of the prospect's words as you understand them.

For example, you might say, "Let me see if I understand you," then repeat in your words what you heard the prospect say. End with something like, "Do I have the right idea?"

Sometimes you can read a little more into what the buyer actually said, like, "You're saying that if we could get the material to you within two weeks, we have a deal, right?"

There is potential danger lurking behind the use of questions designed to check on what the prospect said or meant. You have to be very careful to avoid any implication that the prospect can't express himself well or is just a little stupid. You would probably be antagonized if a salesperson said, "I think what you mean to say is . . ." or "I just don't follow you," or "Let me see if I can rephrase what you said."

As the salesperson, you can afford to appear stupid for failing to understand, but don't risk making the prospects feel you think they're not too bright.

Ask, Then Suggest

The rising popularity in the use of questions by professional salespeople is undoubtedly related to the human dislike for being TOLD anything. Humans don't mind getting answers to questions, however. The older selling strategy of TELLING the prospect what he should do is being replaced by the use of probing questions to draw the prospect's wants and desires into the open where they become questions to be answered.

Here is an example of how a salesperson might follow up on the information obtained by probing questions. "From what you have told me, it seems that the question is, can we reduce the noise level in this area and still maintain or increase your present output. Would you agree?" When the prospect agrees that this is a fair analysis of the question, all the salesperson has to do is answer the question and the sale is in the works.

But what if the prospect says that is not the question? The prospect just identifies the right question and the salesperson tries to answer it.

People prefer to get suggestions, rather than being TOLD what to do. So the professional salesperson, after asking probing questions, might say, "From what you have told me, do you mind if I make a suggestion?" Not many prospects would refuse to listen to a suggestions, but they might emotionally reject a statement like, "You should install this equipment."

Questions to Get Action

Asking questions is a favorite way to start closing the sale as discussed in Chapter 10. The questions are designed to lead the buyer into making decisions which will result in the sale. Here are some examples.

"Which model do you like best?"
"How soon would you have to get delivery?"
"Would three gross be sufficient or should we increase it to four?"

The salesperson normally wants to avoid asking questions in a form that sounds threatening to the buyer or will raise the anxiety level to the extent that the buyer calls the sales negotiation off. On the other hand, there may be circumstances where it's worth a gamble to get the prospect to take action. If the sale isn't going anywhere anyway, perhaps a jolt will pay off, like, "What would happen if this machine would break down tomorrow?" or, "How would your superiors react if the safe you bought failed to protect your records during a fire?" or, "These tires could blow out on your next trip. How would you feel if your family were in the wreck that might result?"

Watch Your Language!

You must be careful in phrasing your questions so you don't antagonize the buyer. The question, "Why did you paint that such a strange color?" is not apt to get a friendly reply since it suggests a lack of taste. A safer way to get the same information is to ask the buyer what she thinks about the subject, like, "How do you feel about the present color scheme you have?"

How you ask the question can have a lot to do with the reaction that follows. The salesperson who asks an office manager, "Who bought this silly duplicator anyway?" shouldn't be surprised when the manager says, "I did. Now if you'll excuse me, I have some other salespeople to see."

A pleasant manner is helpful in a salesperson but attempts at humor can be dangerous. It's too easy to offend someone with the wrong kind of humor or at the expense of someone who can affect the sale. "Where did you get that sofa, at a rummage sale?" might be humorous to others but not to the person who owns it.

Avoid comments that infer the buyer is a bit stupid in his views or that your views are much superior. "Hey, that idea went out in the 60's." Compare that with, "I can understand your point, Mr. Steller. Many had that view until the bonding cements were greatly improved. Now even the luxury homes going up in Broadmoor have their sheating bonded with cement instead of just nails."

While it's a good general rule to keep questions impersonal, don't hesitate to ask a personal question if it will help. Just don't make it critical. "I'm curious, Mr. Falk. Why do you insist on that specific window frame in the specifications?"

Buyers will talk about problems and even bad decisions in answer to your questions. Be supportive, not critical of the information you get on questioning. "I can understand how you feel . . ." "That was a good move on your part."

The Customer is Center Stage

Old time selling cast the salesperson as the performer, on stage. The customers sat back and listened to the performance. Today's selling strategies put the prospects on stage with the salesperson cast in the role of adviser and counselor. Both the prospect and the salesperson participate in the interview, two-way communication.

The most important answer: "Yes, I'll buy!"

As with all successful interviews, questions are the key to the quality of the responses. When salespeople have mastered the art of questioning, they induce the prospects to reveal their needs, recognize their desires and form their own conclusions.

If the questioning is successful, the conclusions are to accept the salesperson's proposition . . . to buy!

12

How to Listen Effectively in Sales Negotiation

Listening Is a Sales Negotiating Skill

THE ABILITY to listen, REALLY listen, is an important characteristic of any successful sales negotiator. Only by listening carefully to what the customer is saying can the sales negotiator hope to gain the information on the buyer's needs, wants, emotions and establish honest goals for the negotiation.

We have stressed the importance of using probing questions in the sales negotiation, but their value will be largely wasted if the salesperson fails to listen correctly to the answers.

Our training in schools concentrates on the reading, writing and speaking phases of our communication activity. Yet studies made by the University of Minnesota show that the communications activity breaks down into approximately these proportions: 9% in writing; 16% in reading; 30% in talking and 45% in listening. We get little instruction in improving the skill that consumes most of our communication time, listening. Educators assumed that listening required no special skills and that when we weren't talking, we were automatically listening. Studies show that that isn't necessarily true and even when our ears are physically hearing, we might not be mentally listening.

Listening Is Important In Any Profession

Developing better listening skills is important to anyone who must react to what a client, patient, negotiating party or sales prospect is saying. So we find courses in listening now offered in many college curricula based on findings of communication authorities. Shorter, intense courses in listening are also being taught business executives and salespeople to improve their listening power.

Listening during the sales negotiation involves the observation of two basic types of clues . . . verbal and behavioral. Verbal clues are the words the buyer uses as well as the voice intonations and inflections. They are the answers the buyer gives to the salesperson's questions we discussed in Chapter 11. How the words are said can give them different meanings.

Behavioral clues, commonly called "body language," are the meanings you can gain from the buyer's facial expressions, eye contact, posture and gestures. Single clues, words or body actions, take on added significance when interpreted together.

THE BIG 3 LISTENING PROBLEMS

Sales negotiators have the same problems in listening as everyone else. But since their careers depend upon getting the right information on which to take action, it is more important that they recognize the listening problems and do something to reduce them.

Researchers on listening say that the major problems everyone, including salespeople, has in listening fit into these three primary areas:

1. They don't pay attention. Good listening takes effort and we all tend to avoid work when we can.

Listening requires blocking out the other things we want to do while the buyer is talking. It's too easy, for example, to think about what to say next instead of paying attention to what the buyer is saying.

The clergy knows that everyone watching the pulpit intently is not necessarily listening to the sermon. Teachers, speakers and experienced buyers also know that the glazed eyes and the occasional nods give the faker away. Salespeople who know the value of showing an interest in what the buyer is saying, are equally guilty of faking listening on occasions while thinking up additional selling strategies to use when the buyer finishes talking.

A good fake is probably better than paying no attention to the buyer at all, but it could result in your failing to hear clues that could guide you to the sale.

2. They miss the real point. Salespeople might actually listen carefully, concentrating on facts, even keeping them in mind or writing them down, and still not be getting the real keys to the sale.

Facts out of context can cause misunderstanding or result in wrong conclusions. Sometimes, too, salespeople become more interested in the buyer's accent, surroundings, clothing or mannerisms and miss the points he or she is making.

3. They let emotions interfere. Emotion is a barrier to real comprehension. It makes us hostile or too enthusiastic about the buyer's point of view. Emotions are difficult to control by nature. But when the salespeople realize what they can do to destroy a sale, they can recognize their emotions taking over and say to themselves, "Hold it! I'd better calm down and look for the real information I can use to make this sale."

3 OTHER LISTENING PROBLEMS

Here are three other listening problems in addition to the basic three that interfere with good listening for anyone. They are particularly dangerous traps for sales negotiators, however, because they can result in missing crucial information that can be used to win the sale. Knowing that they exist is the first step to correcting these problems. Since the solution is as simple in most cases as "don't do that," you should be well on your way to improving your listening power now that you are able to recognize what's probably keeping you from being an effective listener.

4. They are distracted. Some distractions make good listening impossible, like phones ringing, noisy surroundings or the entrance of an attractive secretary. But with a little practice, any salesperson can learn to tune out most of the distractions while the buyer is talking.

5. They step on the buyer's statements. You can't listen to what buyers will say if you don't give them a chance to say it. Poor listeners are so anxious to get on with their own talking that they "step on the lines" of the speaker as the actors describe it. They cut in before the person talking has a chance to complete the sentence or the thought.

Salespeople have special knowledge and enthusiasm that impels them to "set the buyers right" rather than hearing them out. In the days before questioning and listening became popular selling tools for persuading people to buy, salespeople felt they had to overwhelm the customer with one-way communication, dominating the conversation, stepping on any attempt by the buyer to talk except on the salesperson's terms.

Today's professional salesperson knows the value of getting prospects to talk, so it should be obvious that effective listening requires that we let them talk and not cut them off in mid-sentence.

From your own experience with people who cut you off when you try to carry on a conversation, you know that your reaction is to quit talking. Buyers do the same when salespeople show their lack of interest by cutting them off while they're talking.

Professional sales negotiators who are also effective listeners, actually use questions like those we discussed in Chapter 11 to KEEP the buyers talking.

6. They misuse higher thought speed. People think at much faster speeds than they can talk . . . or listen. Most people speak from 120 to 160 words a minute, yet we think at four to five times that speed according to the communication experts. The difference between the speed of speech and thought is a definite handicap to listening. It contributes to lack of attention, allowing distractions to interfere and cutting off the buyers before they finish.

Listening salespeople have time to think ahead to what they assume the buyer is going to say, so they are tempted to cut the buyer off before he finishes. They also have extra thinking time to come up with something to say they may feel is more important than what the buyer is saying and are tempted to start talking before the buyer is finished.

Experts say that we shouldn't try to synchronize our thought speed to the buyer's talking speed because that would be impossible. Instead, we should concentrate on using our thought speed advantage to better comprehension of what the buyer is saying, getting to the real point, and formulating a plan of action to take on the basis of what we are hearing . . . WITHOUT cutting the buyer off.

As brought out in Listening Problem 5, you want to keep the buyers talking as long as they contribute to your strategy for closing the sales negotiation successfully.

11 WAYS TO IMPROVE YOUR LISTENING SKILL

Good courses and seminars on listening skills are available to salespeople in most areas. Many companies include listening as one of the topics in their sales training programs. These courses may take from three hours to several days to complete depending upon the amount of practice and drill involved.

We suggest that you attend one of these courses or seminars when they are conveniently available. They will not only help improve your sales negotiation skills, they will help you in communicating with the many other people involved in your life . . . especially your family, friends and business associates.

We will discuss some of the guidelines the professional listening courses bring out to make you a better listener. We cannot provide the valuable practice drills available in these courses, unfortunately.

But if you conscientiously practice these suggestions when talking with anyone, on ANY occasion, you will definitely improve your listening attitude and skills in your sales negotiation.

1. Determine that you WILL listen. The typical salespeople feel uncomfortable when not talking, so they tend to take over the sales negotiation interview with their own talking, forcing the buyer to listen.

Talking is obviously essential, and saying the right things is important. But seldom will salespeople need to talk over half the time.

Letting the buyers talk accomplishes valuable learning about their needs, wants and desires. Some salespeople try to limit their talking to a minute at a time before asking the buyer a question. A minute sounds like a short time, but time it with your watch and you'll find that a lot of words can be said . . . and wasted . . . in that interval.

If buyers try to cut into your presentation, let them. If you don't, they'll probably not hear what you continue to say anyway. Few things are as interesting to hear as what we're waiting to say.

When the buyer asks a question, pause before giving the answer if you can. Wait a few seconds to show that you consider the question a fair one and you want to give a deserving answer. In fact, you will probably give a better answer by waiting a few seconds. By waiting, you also are more sure that the buyer has finished talking and is ready to listen to your answer.

2. Pay attention. A lamp doesn't light until someone flips the switch. You can't really listen to a buyer until you flip your attention switch. Giving full attention to most things is difficult because of distractions or other thoughts that crowd us.

To listen to what the buyer is saying, you have to subordinate the other things that are crying to be heard in your mind. This might take some pretty drastic discipline at times, like mentally telling yourself, "Hey, if you want to sell this prospect you better keep listening to what he's saying!"

Buyers expect salespeople to listen to them when they talk. They hate to be ignored, and if they are, they counter by ignoring the salesperson in return. Even when you might consider the buyer's words unimportant, acknowledge them by giving signs of attention like a word, question, gesture or facial expression. If the buyer stops talking because of your apparent inattention, you lose your main source of information for making the sale as well as a receptive mind to your attempts at persuasion.

3. Ignore distractions. Distractions are deadly to listening, yet they can be minimized with conscious effort and practice. Distractions tend to affect listening to the degree in which we are interested in the subject.

Like the experienced radio operator, we can learn how to tune out the static and keep what the buyer is saying coming through.

Even when interest is low, we can consciously refrain from paying undue attention to the prospect's mannerisms, clothes, speech, voice, or pipe. Some are more difficult, like a ringing telephone or another visitor, but try to take them in stride and get back to listening as long as the buyer talks.

Do what you can physically to minimize the distractions. Step in or move your chair closer to hear better. Ask if a door can be closed to offending noise. Ask, "Can we go someplace where we will not be interrupted for at least fifteen minutes?"

Some professional salespeople, when they have an important proposal to present to a buyer and have had experience with interrupting phone calls previously, have successfully asked the client to hold phone calls so the proposition can be delivered uninterrupted. These requests, while seemingly bold to ask a customer, actually give added stature to you proposition and usually impress the buyer favorably. Obviously, the key to this kind of request is to have something important enough to warrant the buyer's full, uninterrupted attention.

4. Control your emotions. Don't let your emotions close your mind to listening. Some buyers could easily raise our tempers with emotional words or actions, especially with unfair complaints or accusations. Treat each emotional outburst like you do any objection and let the buyers talk. Even encourage them to talk to get the venom out of their system. Your emotions will tell you not to take that abuse, to fight back, to tell the buyer off. But keep cool. Remember to keep listening for clues that will help you make that sale. You might say, "I can see why you would be upset. Would you tell me what happened?" As the buyer talks and lets off steam, listen for clues that all is not lost, like "Your deliveries are usually good, but this time . . " or "Even if your merchandise does cost less . . ." You won't hear these clues on which you could build a compromise if your own emotions are out of control.

Excitement over the possibilities of making a sale is an emotion that can also get in the way of listening. Over-anxiety and impatience on the part of the salesperson make the buyer cautious, too. Control your excitement without destroying your enthusiasm. Steer your enthusiasm into listening and responding to what the buyer is saying.

5. Listen for keys to the sale. While listening, mentally ask yourself, "What is the buyer saying that I can use to bring this sale about?" The sale depends on satisfying the prospect's problems, needs, wants and desires, so you want to listen for key signals of these in what the prospect says.

Salespeople are seeking information from the buyers that will guide them into matching their product or service to explicit needs, wants and desires.

Listen particularly for the buyer's use of personal pronouns like our, we, you and us.

6. Focus on ideas. A good listener searches for the main ideas rather than facts alone. Facts are important, of course, like size, quantities, colors, etc. But the salesperson must weigh one fact against the other to get their relationships, a central theme on which the sale could be made.

Try to find the drives the buyer is exposing. A couple may show interest in a new sofa and suggest facts like size, color and style. But their actions and comments may also tell the listening salesperson that they would prefer to have prestige styling rather than lowest price.

Once you uncover some basic drives in the buyer, you can concentrate your negotiation skills on them.

7. Listen beyond the words. People don't always say what they really mean about what they want or their desire to buy. Most people are defensive in buying.

Salespeople must listen for clues on why the prospect is not buying and not take statements like "I can't afford it" at face value. Such a statement frequently means, "You haven't convinced me yet."

Probing questions by the salesperson can usually bring out the real reasons for resistance so they can be handled.

8. Practice listening. We've shown that good listening takes concentration. The ability to concentrate on what other people are saying can be improved through practice. One easy way is to concentrate on listening to anyone, not necessarily a customer, several minutes each hour, then trying to recall what they said. Practice the reactions we've discussed to keep the person talking.

Ask questions. Listening closely to radio and television speakers is also good practice for concentration, avoiding distractions and retention of the message.

9. Listen and persuade. When listening to a speaker on the podium, we seldom have an opportunity to become involved in the communication. But the two-way communication between salespeople and buyers permits the salespeople to participate and persuade the buyer.

As we have seen, you can persuade merely by listening attentively. But you can also inject the questions and comments covered in the other sections to make more effective persuasive points.

10. Put yourself in the buyer's place. When you can relate to the buyer's problems, you are in a better position to solve them to his satisfaction. By listening and asking questions, salespeople develop empathy with the buyers. Empathy is defined as "mentally entering into the feeling and spirit of a person," the best way to arrive at understanding.

Studies show that people stop buying from a firm that seemingly ignores them and their desires. Listening will go a long way toward keeping old customers and adding new ones.

11. Use feedback. Simple games have been used to show that a group of people can listen to the same thing and come up with a variety of meanings and facts. While this can make a party game fun, it should make the sales-person aware of the importance of really understanding what the prospect is saying.

The best technique for getting this result is to repeat back to the buyers what you think they just said. This is called feedback. You might say, "Now let me see if I understand what you will need ." If the buyer doesn't agree that this is what he had in mind, he will correct your interpretation. You avoid wasted time and wrong solutions to the problem. The buyer appreciates your interest and obvious determination to help.

Use Time Lag Constructively

Your mind travels at least four times faster than the average buyer talks. So you have thinking time to spare while listening to the buyer talking. What you do with that spare time determines your efficiency as a listener. A poor listener starts out trying to listen, but then finds there's time to spare and lets the mind wander to other things not related to making the sale. Meanwhile, what the buyer is saying gets lost.

A good listener knows what can happen and takes definite action to avoid wandering off. Here are some suggestions for using the time lag constructively.

1. Anticipate what the buyer is going to talk about. Ask yourself, "What is the point he will make?"

2. Summarize mentally what the buyer has been saying. What are the key points?

3. Evaluate what the buyer is saying. Question the facts. Ask yourself, "Are the facts true? Is there any prejudice involved? Is this the whole picture or just the part that proves his point?"

4. If you are listening to an answer to your question, is the buyer being evasive?

5. Listen to the words, but mentally listen to the non-verbal signs that could have more meaning, like the changing tones and volume of the voice, the facial expressions, emphasis, gestures and body movements.

Listen to the Body Language, Too!

In addition to the verbal clues, we mentioned earlier the sales negotiator needs to consider the buyer's behavioral clues as well. In recent years, these behavioral clues have received a considerable amount of identification and study. They are commonly referred to as "body language" because they are often as important as the verbal language when communicating with other persons.

There have been numerous books and articles written by psychologists and other experts on body language and its interpretation. We suggest that you read the books listed in the Bibliography and magazine articles on the subject to get a feel for the types of actions to look for and how to interpret them in your prospects and customers.

There are mixed feelings on the value of body language in sales negotiations, however. Some experienced negotiators point out that experienced and proficient buyers are also good actors. Like poker players, they can fake their body language to mislead salespeople into more concessions.

Let's identify some of the more recognizable elements of body language that buyers can exhibit. You will be able to add to the list from your own experience and your readings on the subject.

Signals That You Are Welcome

Acceptance of the appointment
Pleasing expression when greeted
Offered handshake
Invited to sit down
Stops present activity when you come in
Keeps head turned toward you
Keeps direct eye contact
Closes door
Asks not to be disturbed by staff or phone
Agrees to watch audio-visual presentation

Signals of Interest

Alert facial expressions
Leans forward in chair, hands relaxed
Reads items offered like literature
Reads label on product
Asks questions about product or service
Offers statements about your firm and product
Nods head as you talk
Enters into your presentation with comments
Answers questions willingly
Keeps in direct eye contact
Strokes chin thoughtfully
Mouth slightly open

Signals of Lack of Interest

Dull facial expressions
Slumps in chair
Talks about other topics
Turns away to do other things
Looks around the room, at desk, out window
Makes no comments
Asks no questions
Doodles
Hums to self
Looks at watch or clock repeatedly
Taps fingers and feet
Looks at phone as if expecting it to ring
Makes phone calls on other subjects
Takes phone calls and chats
Calls in secretary and gives other assignments
Voice tone exhibits restlessness
Makes excuse to end call early

Signals of Hostility

Pounds desk with hand
Rising voice inflection
Clenched jaw
Clenched fists
Arms folded
Body gestures tight, jerky
Brows knit and eyes squinting
Rubs nose
Leans forward with palms down
Points finger or object at you
Laughs at salesperson's serious statements, especially price
Shifts papers and objects forcefully
Ends call abruptly
Asks you to leave

What To Do About the Buyer's Signals

What should you do when you recognize a behavioral clue?

Just as with verbal clues, recognizing them is the most important step. After that you follow your experience and apply your selling skills.

Signals of welcome and interest naturally tell you you're on the right track, so alter you plan to go for the trial close early. Don't wait too long or the interest may dry up.

With signals of reduced interest, do something to increase the buyer's interest as mentioned in Chapter 8, like participating in your demonstration, asking questions, using stories of how others used your products, increasing your own enthusiasm.

When you begin to get signals of hostility, ask probing questions to get at the reasons the buyer feels as he does. It may be something you can correct and bring the buyer back into your fold. Your techniques for handling resistance and objections like those discussed in Chapter 9 will suggest questions and procedures to take.

Even when the signals tell you you're fighting a lost cause, recognizing them early permits you to take your leave and invest the time you save on a more receptive buyer.

Work on Your Own Body Language

Body language works for both parties in negotiations. So think about the image you want to project physically during your sales negotiations. Much has been said about the importance of enthusiasm on the part of the salesperson in the outcome of the sale. Enthusiasm is catching, but not so much as the lack of it. The buyer is also watching your body language and how you react to his suggestions and counter proposals.

When you are aware of how body language works and what the actions mean to the buyer, you can learn your part like the stage actor to project the image you want the buyer to see. Read the books on body language from the standpoint of how you can affect other people as well as your prospects and customers with your nonverbal strategies. The suggestions may come in handy in your family and business negotiations as well as in selling!

Practice! Practice!

All of your skillful presentation, your penetrating questions to probe for hidden needs and desires of the buyer, lose their potential for selling success if you fail to match them with equal skill in listening to the buyer's responses.

There is a price to pay for good listening habits. Tests have shown that intense listening is characterized by increased heart action, faster circulation and increased body temperature. And we all know that listening when we would rather be talking is an emotional strain. But in selling, listening pays off as a good investment.

The suggestions in this Chapter for developing more effective listening skills have put other salespeople into higher levels of professional accomplishment. But they are just interesting reading if you fail to use them to improve your own listening skills that will increase the effectiveness of your sales negotiations.

Epilogue

You Are a Professional Sales Negotiator

BEFORE you began reading this book, you undoubtedly considered yourself a professional salesperson. You had already developed the required skills and knowledge to determine customer needs and desires and to persuade them to buy your product or service to satisfy them.

You are still that professional salesperson. But because you have added negotiation strategies and tactics to your selling expertise, you will now operate at a higher level of selling competency . . . as a Sales Negotiator!

I don't expect you to order new business cards that say Sales Negotiator instead of Sales Representative or whatever your current title. And I'm sure that you won't get an automatic raise by adding SN after your name.

But I AM sure that you will make more sales and earn more money after you start using some of the many strategies, tactics and ideas for sales negotiation we covered here.

That's the bottom line all professionals hope for when they put forth the effort to reach a higher level of compentency!

Developing Your Negotiating Skills

In Part I you learned about the specific strategies and tactics used by professional business and government negotiators that are particularly adaptable to selling situations.

You may have read other books on general negotiation, or you may have attended a negotiation seminar. If so, you recognized the fact that we selected and concentrated on just those elements of good negotiation practice that SALESPEOPLE could use effectively to close more sales.

There was no need to read or listen to stories on how business, labor, and government negotiators negotiate, trying to decide whether the same ideas would work for you in a selling situation.

This book saved you all that time, effort, confusion and trial and error by selecting and reinforcing those negotiation strategies and tactics that will work for you in improving your selling results!

You Know the Buyer's Game Plan

After studying Chapter 2, you are now better prepared to cope with the tactics of buyers who have read a book or taken the typical course on negotiation that shows them how to get a lower price and win more concessions from salespeople.

You are now aware of their game plan, so you have time to prepare your defenses against any of their anticipated tactics.

You've Always Been a Negotiator

Shortly after you began reading this book, you undoubtedly said, "Hey, I've been using that negotiation technique all along in my sales plan." And you're right. Professional salespeople are negotiators by necessity. In fact, you've been negotiating with other people all your life! The difference is that now you have a better appreciation of the negotiating power you have going into a sales situation.

In Chapter 3 you learned how to take advantage of the strengths you have and how to develop added strengths you can use effectively during the sales negotiation.

In Chapter 4, you learned about special strategies and tactics professional negotiators use in other fields that you can adapt to your own use as a sales professional.

More important, each example and each suggested action was related to selling situations. This made it easier to evaluate the principles and to apply them more quickly to your own sales planning and operation.

Integrating Your Negotiating and Selling Skills

As important as it is to learn about negotiation strategies and tactics, they will never result in more sales for you until you integrate them with your existing professional selling skills. That's why Part II is perhaps the most important part of this book. Without it, this would be just another book on negotiation even though designed specifically for salespeople.

Part II selects the most effective selling techniques used by today's professional salespeople at each stage of the sale and shows how specific negotiation techniques can be integrated with them.

Here is where this book's unique concept of SELLING THROUGH NEGOTIATION comes together!

A Review of the Best In Selling Techniques

If you are an experienced salesperson, you recognized the professional persuasive selling techniques that are summarized in Part II. But you appreciated having them tailored to and reinforced by the negotiation strategies and tactics you have learned here. This makes it easier to put them into operation in your own selling situations.

If you are relatively new in selling, Part II offers an added benefit. It provides an opportunity to review the best selling techniques used by today's professional salespeople so you can integrate your new negotiating skills with them. For best sales results, the two skills must be equally professional.

These techniques were collected by the author after many years of training salespeople, listening to top sales trainers of leading companies and observing how the super-salespeople sell.

Question and Listen Effectively

Questioning and listening skills have proved essential in all forms of negotiation. They have also been recognized in recent years as highly important for effective selling. That makes them doubly essential skills for sales negotiation.

In Part II, we demonstrated how questions could be used in all steps of the sales negotiation. Then we added Part III to give additional emphasis to developing more expertise in both questioning and listening.

Consider This Your HANDBOOK for Sales Negotiation

As the cover indicates, and as we recommended before, you should consider this book your HANDBOOK for Sales Negotiation. There's no way you can remember all the negotiation strategies and tactics you have read about and how to use them to improve your chances of making more sales.

Come back to the various Chapters for review and refinement as you gain experience and expertise in applying what you have learned about negotiation.

You may want to improve your opening of the sales interview or the presentation and closing stages, for example. Or you may run into a particular objection or resistance problem. If so, come back and review the sales negotiation tactics to see if one of them you're not now using might be helpful.

And Practice, Practice, Practice!

None of the great ideas in this book for improving your sales negotiation skills will do you any good until you USE them! Make a commitment NOW to try them out as soon as possible.

You can't use them all at once, of course, and some may not fit your selling situation. But you can start using the ones you would feel most comfortable in using, or the ones that should work particularly well on a sales proposal coming up. After you try a few negotiation strategies and find they work, you will want to add more and more.

Like the learning of any skill, practice is most important. Make a conscious effort to add and repeat negotiation tactics at various stages of your sales presentations. A review of Part II will help you here.

When you try a new negotiation technique, evaluate its results after the sales interview. What went well? What should you have done differently? How will you treat the same situation next time?

What You've Learned Can Change Your Life!

A major objective of this book was to help you close more sales through your improved negotiation skill. That should improve your standing with the firm, your prestige among fellow workers and, of course, your income. While that's a worthwhile objective, the value doesn't stop there.

I'm sure that your experience from now on will be much the same as mine has been since I began to study negotiation. You will find that you use your new negotiation skill and knowledge in your personal affairs as well as on your selling job.

You're a consumer as well as a salesperson, and now that you know how professional buyers negotiate, you'll find yourself coming out better when negotiating with your own merchants and suppliers.

You're probably on a committee or two in your community, and you'll find yourself using your negotiation skills to help move the rest of the committee or one of its members around to your view.

Finally, you will find that these same techniques can work on members of your family and friends, too. But be gentle! Remember what we said about the ideal win-win results of negotiation?

Be particulatly aware, however, that your spouse or friend might have more negotiating power than you anticipated . . . and KNOWS how to use it! To be fully prepared, better review Part I again.

Thanks for spending this time with us, and good SELLING THROUGH NEGOTIATION!